AAT

Qualifications and Credit Framework (QCF)

AQ2013
LEVEL 4 DIPLOMA IN ACCOUNTING

(QCF)

QUESTION BANK

Budgeting

2014 Edition

For assessments from September 2014

Second edition June 2014
ISBN 9781 4727 0938 7

Previous edition
ISBN 9781 4727 0351 4

British Library Cataloguing-in-Publication Data
A catalogue record for this book is available from the British Library

Published by
BPP Learning Media Ltd
BPP House
Aldine Place
London W12 8AA

www.bpp.com/learningmedia

Printed in the United Kingdom by Martins of Berwick
Sea View Works
Spittal
Berwick-Upon-Tweed
TD15 1RS

CONTENTS

Introduction   v

Question and Answer bank

A NOTE ABOUT COPYRIGHT

Dear Customer

What does the little © mean and why does it matter?

Your market-leading BPP books, course materials and e-learning materials do not write and update themselves. People write them: on their own behalf or as employees of an organisation that invests in this activity. Copyright law protects their livelihoods. It does so by creating rights over the use of the content.

Breach of copyright is a form of theft – as well being a criminal offence in some jurisdictions, it is potentially a serious breach of professional ethics.

With current technology, things might seem a bit hazy but, basically, without the express permission of BPP Learning Media:

- Photocopying our materials is a breach of copyright

- Scanning, ripcasting or conversion of our digital materials into different file formats, uploading them to facebook or emailing them to your friends is a breach of copyright

You can, of course, sell your books, in the form in which you have bought them – once you have finished with them. (Is this fair to your fellow students? We update for a reason.) Please note the e-products are sold on a single user licence basis: we do not supply 'unlock' codes to people who have bought them secondhand.

And what about outside the UK? BPP Learning Media strives to make our materials available at prices students can afford by local printing arrangements, pricing policies and partnerships which are clearly listed on our website. A tiny minority ignore this and indulge in criminal activity by illegally photocopying our material or supporting organisations that do. If they act illegally and unethically in one area, can you really trust them?

INTRODUCTION

This is BPP Learning Media's AAT Question Bank for Budgeting. It is part of a suite of ground-breaking resources produced by BPP Learning Media for the AAT's assessments under the Qualification and Credit Framework.

The Budgeting assessment will be **computer assessed**. As well as being available in the traditional paper format, this **Question Bank is available in an online environment** containing tasks similar to those you will encounter in the AAT's testing environment. BPP Learning Media believe that the best way to practise for an online assessment is in an online environment. However, if you are unable to practise in the online environment you will find that all tasks in the paper Question Bank have been written in a style that is as close as possible to the style that you will be presented with in your online assessment.

This Question Bank has been written in conjunction with the BPP Text, and has been carefully designed to enable students to practise all of the learning outcomes and assessment criteria for the units that make up Budgeting. It is fully up to date as at June 2014 and reflects both the AAT's unit guide and the sample assessment(s) provided by the AAT.

This Question Bank contains these key features:

- Tasks corresponding to each chapter of the Text. Some tasks are designed for learning purposes, others are of assessment standard.

- The AAT's sample assessments and answers for Budgeting and further BPP practice assessments.

The emphasis in all tasks and assessments is on the practical application of the skills acquired.

VAT

You may find tasks throughout this Question Bank that need you to calculate or be aware of a rate of VAT. This is stated at 20% in these examples and questions.

Approaching the assessment

When you sit the assessment it is very important that you follow the on screen instructions. This means you need to carefully read the instructions, both on the introduction screens and during specific tasks.

When you access the assessment you should be presented with an introductory screen with information similar to that shown below (taken from the introductory screen from the AAT's AQ2013 Sample Assessment for Budgeting)

Please note that in this practice test only your responses to tasks 1, 2, 3, 4, 6 and 7 are marked. Equivalents of tasks 5 and 8 will be human marked in the live assessment.

Where the date is relevant, it is given in the task data.
Minus signs should be used to indicate negative numbers.

You must use a full stop to indicate a decimal point.
For example, write 100.57 NOT 100,57 or 100 57

You may use a comma to indicate a number in the thousands, but you don't have to.
For example, 10000 and 10,000 are both OK.

Other indicators are not compatible with the computer-marked system.

Complete all 8 tasks.

The actual instructions may vary so it is very important you read the instructions on the introductory screen and apply them in the assessment. You don't want to lose marks when you know the correct answer just because you have not entered it in the right format.

In general, the rules set out in the AAT Sample Assessments for the subject you are studying for will apply in the real assessment, but you should again read the information on this screen in the real assessment carefully just to make sure. This screen may also confirm the VAT rate used if applicable.

A full stop is needed to indicate a decimal point. We would recommend using minus signs to indicate negative numbers and leaving out the comma signs to indicate thousands, as this results in a lower number of key strokes and less margin for error when working under time pressure. Having said that, you can use whatever is easiest for you as long as you operate within the rules set out for your particular assessment.

You have to show competence throughout the assessment and you should therefore complete all of the tasks. Don't leave questions unanswered.

In the Budgeting assessment the extended writing tasks will be human marked. In this case you are given a blank space to enter your answer into. You are told in the assessments which tasks these are (note: there may be none if all answers are marked by the computer).

If these involve calculations, it is a good idea to decide in advance how you are going to lay out your answers to such tasks by practicing answering them on a word document, and certainly you should try all such tasks in this question bank and in the AAT's environment using the sample/practice assessments.

When asked to fill in tables, or gaps, never leave any blank even if you are unsure of the answer. Fill in your best estimate.

Note that for some assessments where there is a lot of scenario information or tables of data provided (eg tax tables), you may need to access these via 'pop-ups'. Instructions will be provided on how you can bring up the necessary data during the assessment.

Finally, take note of any task specific instructions once you are in the assessment. For example you may be asked to enter a date in a certain format or to enter a number to a certain number of decimal places.

Remember you can practise the BPP questions in this question bank in an online environment on our dedicated AAT Online page. On the same page is a link to the current AAT Sample Assessments as well.

If you have any comments about this book, please email ianblackmore@bpp.com or write to Ian Blackmore, AAT Range Manager, BPP Learning Media Ltd, BPP House, Aldine Place, London W12 8AA.

Question bank

Chapter 1 Cost classification

Task 1.1

Match the departments in the first column with their purpose in the second column.
(CBT instructions: Click on a box in the left column, then on one in the right column. To remove a line, click on it.)

Department
Sales team
Finance department
Facilities team
HR department
Marketing team

Purpose
Prepares the draft financial statements of the organisation
Ensures the business manages its staff correctly, including adhering to employment law
Promotes the organisation in the market place
Finds and secures new customers
Responsible for decisions concerning the buildings from which the organisation trades

Task 1.2

Select an appropriate budget in which to place each cost listed below.

Cost	Budget	
Market research survey		▼
Wages of factory workers		▼
Recruitment advertisement for a new finance director in an accountancy magazine		▼
Raw material costs		▼
Salary of marketing director		▼

Picklist:

Administrative overheads budget
Production budget
Marketing budget

Task 1.3

Match the functions listed below to the appropriate department.

Function	Department
Prepares accounting information, pays suppliers and staff, chases customers for payment etc	▼
Recruits, develops and disciplines staff, and ensures that employment law is followed by the business	▼
Buys raw materials for use in the production process	▼
Makes sales to new and existing customers	▼
Investigates and responds to customer complaints	▼

Picklist:

After-sales service team
HR department
Purchasing team
Sales team
Finance department

Task 1.4

A company is hosting a dinner event at a function room to entertain clients and is creating the budget for the cost. **Classify each of the costs below in terms of its behaviour as semi-variable, variable, stepped or fixed**.

Cost	Behaviour
Room hire	▼
Food for attendees	▼
Hire of waiting staff – 1 required per 20 attendees	▼

Picklist:

Semi-variable
Variable
Stepped
Fixed

Task 1.5

At a production level of 20,000 units a production cost totals £128,000. At a production level of 32,000 units the same cost totals £204,800.

This a variable cost.

True ☐

False ☐

Task 1.6

From the list below, drag and drop the most appropriate method of apportioning the overheads given in the table between two production departments.

Drag and drop choices:

Number of staff employed
Floor area
Units produced
Average inventory of raw materials held

Cost	Behaviour
Heating	
Rental on storage unit for raw materials	
Canteen expenses	
Depreciation of factory building	

Task 1.7

The following details are available for four types of cost at three activity levels:

	Cost at 10,000 units	Cost at 20,000 units	Cost at 25,000 units
Cost 1	18,000	18,000	18,000
Cost 2	30,000	60,000	60,000
Cost 3	30,000	60,000	75,000
Cost 4	20,000	30,000	35,000

Classify each cost by behaviour (semi-variable, variable, stepped or fixed):

	Cost behaviour	
Cost 1		▼
Cost 2		▼
Cost 3		▼
Cost 4		▼

Picklist:

Semi-variable
Variable
Stepped
Fixed

Task 1.8

A manufacturing business anticipates that its variable production costs and fixed production costs will be £23,000 and £15,000 respectively at a production level of 10,000 units.

Complete the table to show the budgeted total production cost and the budgeted cost per unit at each of the activity levels.

Activity level (units)	Budgeted total production cost £	Budgeted cost per unit £
8,000		
12,000		
15,000		

Task 1.9

Given below are a number of types of cost – classify each one according to its behaviour (semi-variable, variable, stepped or fixed):

	Cost behaviour
Maintenance contract which costs £10,000 annually plus an average of £500 cost per call out	▼
Sales car depreciation based upon miles travelled	▼
Machine consumables cost based on machine hours	▼
Rent for a building that houses the factory, stores and maintenance departments	▼

Picklist:

Semi-variable
Variable
Stepped
Fixed

Task 1.10

Drag and drop an appropriate accounting treatment for each of the costs in the table below:

Costs	Accounting treatment
Servicing of office computer equipment	
Materials wastage in production process	
Depreciation of marketing director's car	
Bonus for finance director	
Sick pay for production workers	

Drag and drop choices:

Direct cost
Charge to production in a labour hour overhead rate
Allocate to administrative overheads
Allocate to marketing overheads

Task 1.11

A business produces one product in its factory which has two production departments, cutting and finishing. There is one service department, stores, which spends 80% of its time servicing the cutting department and the remainder servicing the finishing department.

The expected costs of producing 50,000 units in the following quarter are as follows:

Direct materials	£16.00 per unit
Direct labour	3 hours cutting @ £7.50 per hour
	2 hours finishing @ £6.80 per hour
Cutting overheads	£380,000
Finishing overheads	£280,000
Stores overheads	£120,000

It is estimated that in each of the cost centres 60% of the overheads are variable and the remainder are fixed.

Determine the budgeted cost per unit of production (in £ to the nearest penny) under the following costing methods:

(i) Absorption costing – fixed and variable overheads are to be absorbed on a direct labour hour basis

£ [   ]

(ii) Marginal costing

£ [   ]

Task 1.12

To help decision making during budget preparation, your supervisor has prepared the following estimates of sales revenue and cost behaviour relating to one of your organisation's products for a one-year period.

Activity level	60%	100%
Sales and production (thousands of units)	36	60
	£'000	£'000
Sales	432	720
Production costs – variable and fixed	366	510
Sales, distribution and administration costs – variable and fixed	126	150

The normal level of activity for the current year is 60,000 units, and fixed costs are incurred evenly throughout the year.

There were no inventories of the product at the start of the quarter, in which 16,500 units were made and 13,500 units were sold. Actual fixed costs were the same as budgeted.

You may assume that sales price and variable costs per unit are as budgeted.

(a) **Complete the following using absorption costing:**

	£
Fixed production costs absorbed by the product	
Over/under absorption of fixed product costs	

(b) **Complete the following to find the profit for the quarter using absorption costing**

	£	£
Sales		
Cost of production (no opening inventory)		
Value of inventory produced		
Less value of closing inventory		
Total cost of production		
Subtotal		
Selling, distribution & admin costs		
Variable		
Fixed		
Total selling, distribution and admin costs		
Subtotal		
Over-absorbed/under-absorbed production overhead		
Absorption costing profit		

(c) **Complete the following to find the profit for the quarter using marginal costing:**

	£	£
Sales		
Variable costs of production		
Less value of closing inventory		
Variable cost of sales		
Variable selling, distribution & admin costs		
Total variable costs		
Contribution		
Fixed costs – production		
– selling, distribution & admin		
Total fixed costs		
Marginal costing profit		

Task 1.13

Drampton plc, a computer retailer, has recently taken over Little Ltd, a small company making personal computers (PCs) and servers. Little appears to make all of its profits from servers. Drampton's finance director tells you that Little's fixed overheads are currently charged to production using standard labour hours and gives you their standard cost of making PCs and servers. These are shown below.

Little Ltd: Standard cost per computer

Model	Server	PC
Annual budgeted volume	5	5,000
Unit standard cost		
	£	£
Material and labour	50,000	500
Fixed overhead	4,000	40
Standard cost per unit	54,000	540

The finance director asks for your help and suggests you reclassify the fixed overheads between the two models using activity-based costing. You are given the following information.

- ## Budgeted total annual fixed overheads

	£
Set-up costs	10,000
Rent and power (production area)	120,000
Rent (stores area)	50,000
Salaries of store issue staff	40,000
Total	220,000

Every time Little makes a server, it has to stop making PCs and rearrange the factory layout. The cost of this is shown as set-up costs. If the factory did not make any servers, these costs would be eliminated.

- ## Cost drivers

	Server	PC	Total
Number of set-ups	5	0	5
Number of weeks of production	10	40	50
Floor area of stores (square metres)	400	400	800
Number of issues of inventory	2,000	8,000	10,000

Prepare a note for Drampton's finance director. In the note, you should use the cost drivers to reallocate Little's budgeted total fixed annual overheads between server and PC production and so complete the following:

	Allocated overheads to Server £	Allocated overheads to PC £
Set-up costs		
Rent & power (production area)		
Rent (stores area)		
Salaries of store issue staff		

Chapter 2 Budgetary control systems

Task 2.1

Explain what a budget is, and how it can help management perform their duties.

Task 2.2

For each scenario given below, select the option which best describes the purpose for which the budget is being used in the scenario.

Scenario	Budget use
In order to meet a profit target, the managing director reduces the figure in next year's budget for the staff Christmas party by 25%	▼
The sales director divides the costs for client entertainment between his two sales teams, and gives the managers of those teams permission to spend within that level	▼
A bonus cost of 2% of sales is included in the sales team's budget for the coming period	▼
A retail company is wishing to expand its operations and so includes the rental costs of new shops in its budget	▼
The purchasing manager informs the production manager there will be a world-wide shortage of one type of material in the coming period. The production manager budgets for a different product mix because of this.	▼

Picklist:

Planning
Control
Co-ordination
Authorisation
Motivation

Task 2.3

Explain what the difference is between strategic plans and operational plans.

Explain how the management of a business will set the strategic plans and operational plans for the business.

···

Task 2.4

Briefly explain each of the following terms:

Budget manual

Budget committee

Budget holders

Master budget

···

Task 2.5

Explain the procedures that will be followed from the start of the budgeting process through to the completion of the master budget in a participative budgeting system.

···

Task 2.6

You are the accountant at a manufacturing business, where the managing director already thinks the annual budgeting process wastes too much management time.

Explain to the managing director why it may be appropriate to use a rolling budget and how this works.

···

Task 2.7

You are the new accountant at a manufacturing business. The managing director wants the time spent on preparing the budget to be kept to a minimum. He wants the costs in last year's budget to be adjusted to reflect inflation of costs, and no further work to be done. This is what has been done every year for the last three years.

You discover that some costs included in the budget are always exceeded in practice and so the budget is ignored by some managers.

Write a memo to the managing director explaining why this method of budgeting may be inappropriate, and suggesting an alternative.

···

Chapter 3 Forecasting

Task 3.1

Match each type of data in the first column with an appropriate source for it in the second column. *(CBA instructions: Click on a box in the left column, then on one in the right column. To remove a line, click on it.)*

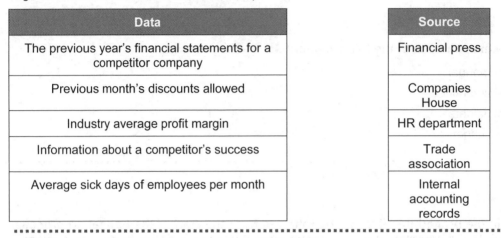

Data	Source
The previous year's financial statements for a competitor company	Financial press
Previous month's discounts allowed	Companies House
Industry average profit margin	HR department
Information about a competitor's success	Trade association
Average sick days of employees per month	Internal accounting records

Task 3.2

Which of the following sets of data is required when preparing the labour usage budget?

Select from

- Forecast labour hours per unit and labour cost per hour
- Forecast production units and labour cost per unit
- Forecast sales units and labour hours per unit
- Forecast production units and labour hours per unit

Task 3.3

If the materials cost per kg and the materials usage budget are already forecast, which other piece of information is required to construct the materials purchases budget?

Select from

- Production budget
- Opening and closing inventory of finished goods
- Sales budget
- Opening and closing inventory of raw materials

Task 3.4

Explain why it is important to produce a capital budget.

....

Task 3.5

Briefly explain what figures would appear in each of the resource budgets that a manufacturing organisation would be likely to prepare and how these figures would be determined.

....

Task 3.6

Forecasting is an important technique for budgeting purposes, however, it has limitations.

Explain the general limitations of forecasting.

....

Task 3.7

Analysis of historical sales data shows a growth trend of 3.5% per quarter. The sales in quarter 1 were 122,000 units.

The time series analysis has also indicated the following seasonal variations:

Quarter 1	+ 6,000 units
Quarter 2	− 8,000 units
Quarter 3	+12,000 units
Quarter 4	−10,000 units

The forecast sales in units for the remaining three quarters are:

Quarter	Forecast sales (units)
Quarter 2	
Quarter 3	
Quarter 4	

....

Task 3.8

The trend figures for sales in units for a business for the four quarters of last year are given below:

Quarter 1	320,000
Quarter 2	325,000
Quarter 3	330,000
Quarter 4	335,000

The seasonal variations are expressed as follows:

Quarter 1	−18%
Quarter 2	+21%
Quarter 3	+7%
Quarter 4	−10%

What are the forecast sales for each of the quarters of next year?

Quarter	Forecast sales (units)
Quarter 1	
Quarter 2	
Quarter 3	
Quarter 4	

Task 3.9

What are the limitations of using time series analysis to forecast figures?

Task 3.10

(a) **Explain the five stages of the product life cycle and how costs and income will alter in each of the five stages.**

(b) **How does knowledge of the product life cycle affect forecasting of future sales?**

Task 3.11

At which stage in the product life cycle is time series analysis most likely to produce a fairly accurate figure for future sales?

Select from:

- Development
- Launch
- Growth
- Maturity
- Decline

....

Task 3.12

The production and sales in units for a business for the next six months are as follows:

	Jan	Feb	Mar	Apr	May	June
Production – units	3,600	2,900	3,200	3,100	3,400	4,000
Sales – units	3,500	3,000	3,000	3,200	3,500	3,800

The variable production costs are £10.50 per unit and the variable selling costs are £3.80 per unit.

Complete the following (to the nearest £):

	Jan	Feb	Mar	Apr	May	Jun
Forecast variable production costs £						
Forecast variable selling costs £						

....

Task 3.13

The direct materials cost for Quarter 1 and Quarter 2 of next year have been estimated in terms of current prices as £657,000 and £692,500 respectively. The current price index for these materials is 126.4 and the price index is estimated as 128.4 for Quarter 1 of next year and 131.9 for Quarter 2.

Complete the following (to the nearest £):

	Quarter 1	Quarter 2
Forecast direct materials costs £		

....

Task 3.14

The production and sales levels for the next three months are estimated as follows:

	Jan	Feb	Mar
Production – units	4,200	4,400	4,500
Sales – units	4,100	4,300	4,650

Variable production costs are currently £25.00 per unit and variable selling costs are £8.00 per unit. The price indices for the production costs and selling costs are currently 135.2 and 140.5 respectively.

The anticipated price indices for production and selling costs for the next three months are given below:

	Jan	Feb	Mar
Production costs index	137.3	139.0	139.6
Selling costs index	141.5	143.0	143.7

Complete the following (to the nearest £)

	Jan	Feb	Mar
Forecast variable production costs £			
Forecast variable selling costs £			

Task 3.15

Last month, a company's electricity bill was £35,000. The cost of electricity will increase with RPI in the coming month, but a prompt payment discount of 5% has also been negotiated.

Last month's machinery maintenance costs were £20,000 when the company had to make 4 call-outs to specialist engineers. The engineers predict that two more machines will fail and require a call-out each in the coming month. Due to rising fuel costs, the cost of a call-out will increase by 5% next month.

Last month's water costs were £62,000 but were unusually high due to a burst pipe (now fixed), which contributed £15,000 to the costs last month. Water prices increase with RPI each month.

The RPI for the last month was 224.6 and the RPI for the coming month is predicted to be 240.3.

The forecast total electricity, machinery maintenance and water costs for the coming month are

£ [   ]

Task 3.16

Last year's rent was £65,000 but will increase next year by 5.5%.

Last year's insurance premium was £15,700 but will increase next year by 10%.

Last year's power costs were £84,000 and these normally increase in line with the average RPI each year.

The average RPI for last year was 166.3 and it is believed that the average RPI for next year will be 171.2.

The forecast fixed costs for next year are

£ [_____]

....

Task 3.17

The costs of a factory maintenance department appear to be partially dependent upon the number of machine hours operated each month. The machine hours and the maintenance department costs for the last six months are given below:

	Machine hours	Maintenance cost £
June	14,200	285,000
July	14,800	293,000
August	15,200	300,000
September	14,500	290,000
October	15,000	298,000
November	14,700	292,000

The estimated variable cost per machine hour is

£ [_____]

The estimated fixed costs of the maintenance department are

£ [_____]

....

Task 3.18

The activity levels and related production costs for the last six months were as follows:

	Activity level units	Production cost £
July	63,000	608,000
August	70,000	642,000
September	76,000	699,000
October	73,000	677,000
November	71,000	652,000
December	68,000	623,000

Complete the following, using the hi lo method to determine the fixed element of the production costs and the variable rate.

State which of the two estimates is likely to be the most accurate and why.

Forecast units	Production costs £
74,000	
90,000	

Task 3.19

If the equation of a straight line defines a semi-variable cost what do the figures representing a and b in the equation mean?

Select from:

- a is the fixed element of cost, b is the variable amount per unit/hour
- a is the variable amount per unit/hour, b is the fixed element of cost
- a is the relevant range of the cost, b is the fixed element of cost
- a is the relevant range of the cost, b is the variable amount per unit/hour

Task 3.20

The linear regression equation for the production costs of a business is:

$$y = 138,000 + 6.4x$$

If production is expected to be 105,000 units in the next quarter what are the anticipated production costs?

Select from:

- £33,000
- £5,156
- £810,000
- £672,000

....

Task 3.21

The linear regression equation for the power costs of a factory is given as follows:

$$y = 80,000 + 0.5x$$

where x is the number of machine hours used in a period.

The anticipated machine hours for the next six months are as follows. **Complete the following giving the forecasts for the power costs.**

	Machine hours	Power costs £
April	380,000	
May	400,000	
June	395,000	
July	405,000	
August	410,000	
September	420,000	

....

Task 3.22

The linear regression equation for the trend of sales in thousands of units per month based upon time series analysis of the figures for the last two years is:

$$y = 3.1 + 0.9x$$

The estimated sales trend for each of the first three months of next year is:

	Sales trend (units)
Month 1	
Month 2	
Month 3	

Task 3.23

A time series analysis of sales volumes each quarter for the last three years, 20X1 to 20X3, has identified the trend equation as follows:

$$y = 400 + 105x$$

where y is the sales volume and x is the time period.

The seasonal variations for each quarter have been calculated as:

Quarter 1	−175
Quarter 2	+225
Quarter 3	+150
Quarter 4	−200

Forecast the sales volume for each quarter of 20X4.

	Sales volume
Quarter 1	
Quarter 2	
Quarter 3	
Quarter 4	

Chapter 4 Budget preparation

Task 4.1

A business has budgeted sales for the next period of 13,800 units of its product. The inventory at the start of the period is 2,100 units and this is to be reduced to 1,500 units at the end of the period.

Which of the following is the production quantity in units for the period?

Select from

- 13,800
- 13,200
- 14,400
- 2,100
- 1,500

Task 4.2

A business is preparing its production budget for the next quarter. It is estimated that 200,000 units of the product can be sold in the quarter and the opening inventory is currently 35,000 units. The inventory level is to be reduced by 30% by the end of the quarter.

Which of the following is the production budget in units for the quarter?

Select from

- 189,500
- 175,500
- 210,500
- 191,923

Task 4.3

A business is preparing its production budget for the next quarter. It will have opening inventory of 1,500 units but wants no closing inventory at the end of the quarter. Sales are likely to exceed production by 20%.

Which of the following is the production budget for the quarter?

Select from

- 1,500 units
- 1,875 units
- 7,500 units
- 9,000 units

Task 4.4

A production process has normal losses of 3% of completed output and production of 16,200 good units is required.

How many units must be produced in total?

Select from

- 16,686
- 16,702
- 486
- 15,714

Task 4.5

The opening inventory and period sales for units of Product A are shown below. Closing inventory is to be 25% of the next period's sales. Sales in period 4 will be 11,200 units.

Complete the production budget for Product A in units.

	Period 1	Period 2	Period 3
Opening inventory	2,700		
Production			
Subtotal			
Sales	10,800	11,500	11,000
Closing inventory			

Task 4.6

The production budget for a product X is shown below for the next three months.

Quality control procedures have shown that 4% of completed production are found to be defective and are unsellable.

Complete the following, showing how many units of product X must be manufactured to allow for the defective items.

	Period 1	Period 2	Period 3
Required units	12,000	11,000	12,500
Manufactured units			

Task 4.7

A business requires 25,400 units of production in a period and each unit requires 5 kg of raw materials in the finished product. The production process has a normal loss of 10% of raw materials during the production process.

What is the total amount of the raw material required for the period?

Select from:

- 114,300 kg
- 26,950 kg
- 28,222 kg
- 141,112 kg

Task 4.8

The production budget for the product is 40,000 units in the quarter.

Each unit of product requires 5 kgs of raw material. Opening inventory of raw material is budgeted to be 30,000 kg and inventory levels are to be reduced by 20% by the end of the quarter.

The material usage budget for the raw material is [   ] kgs

The materials purchasing budget for the raw material is [   ] kgs

Task 4.9

The production budget in units for the next period, period 1, is 32,000, and for period 2 is 35,000.

Each completed unit of the product requires 8 kgs of raw material; however, the production process has a normal loss of 20% of material. Inventory levels of raw materials are held in order to be sufficient to cover 25% of gross production for the following period. The inventory of raw material at the start of period 1 is budgeted to be 64,000 kgs.

The price of each kilogram of raw material is £2.50.

Complete the following:

	Period 1
Materials usage budget in kg	
Materials purchases budget in kg	
Materials purchases budget in £	

Task 4.10

A product requires 18 labour hours for each unit. However 10% of working hours are non-productive.

How many hours must an employee be paid for in order to produce 20 units?

Select from:

- 324 hours
- 400 hours
- 396 hours
- 360 hours

Task 4.11

A business wishes to produce 120,000 units of its product with a standard labour time of 4 hours per unit. The workforce are currently working at 120% efficiency.

How many hours will it take to produce the units required?

Select from:

- 400,000 hours
- 384,000 hours
- 100,000 hours
- 480,000 hours

Task 4.12

	Quarter 1	Quarter 2
Budgeted sales	102,000 units	115,000 units

The inventory of finished goods at the start of quarter 1 is 17,000 units and it is business policy to maintain closing finished goods inventory levels at one-sixth of the following quarter's budgeted sales.

Each unit is forecast to take 5.5 labour hours, however, it is anticipated that during quarter 1, due to technical problems, the workforce will only be working at 95% efficiency.

You are to produce the production budget and the labour usage budget for quarter 1.

For quarter 1, the production budget is [   ] units

For quarter 1, the labour usage budget is [   ] hours

Task 4.13

Using the information given below complete the following budgets for period 1.

	Period 1
Sales budget (£)	
Production budget (units)	
Materials usage budget (kg)	
Materials purchasing budget (kg)	
Labour budget (hours)	
Labour budget (£)	

The sales forecast for period 1 is 3,000 units and for period 2 is 3,400 units. The selling price will be £40 per unit.

The closing inventory of finished goods is to be enough to cover 20% of sales demand for the next period.

3% of production is defective and has to be scrapped with no scrap value.

Each unit of production requires 4 kgs of raw material X and the production process has a normal loss of 10% of the materials input into the process.

It is policy to hold enough raw materials inventory to cover 35% of the following period's production. The inventory level at the start of period 1 is 4,200 kgs of raw material. The material usage for production in period 2 is budgeted as 16,040 kgs.

The standard time for production of one unit is 2 labour hours, however, due to necessary break times only 80% of the time worked is productive. The labour force are paid at a rate of £8 per hour.

••

Task 4.14

The data provided by the sales and production departments for two products is as follows:

	Aye	Bee
Budgeted sales (units) quarter 1	1,500	2,400
Budgeted sales (units) quarter 2	1,500	2,400
Budgeted material per unit (kg)	4	7
Budgeted labour hours per unit	10	7
Opening units of finished inventory	160	300
Closing units of finished inventory (days' sales next quarter)	5 days	5 days
Failure rate of finished production	2%	2.5%
Finance and other costs of holding a unit in inventory per quarter	£6.00	£7.00

The failed units are only discovered after completion of the products and they have no resale value.

Other information available is as follows:

Weeks in each quarter	12 weeks
Days per week	5 days
Hours per week	35 hours
Number of employees	70 employees
Budgeted labour rate per hour	£8.00
Overtime premium for hours worked in excess of 35 hours per week	50%
Budgeted cost of material per kg	£10.00
Opening inventory of raw materials	2,800 kgs
Closing inventory of raw materials (days' current quarter's production)	6 days
Financing and other costs of keeping 1 kg of raw material in inventory per quarter	£2.00

Complete the following for quarter 1

- The number of production days are [ ]

- The closing finished inventory of Aye in units is [ ]

- The closing finished inventory of Bee in units is [ ]

- The labour hours available before overtime has to be paid are [ ]

- Production budget (units): Aye [ ]

  Bee [ ]

- Materials purchases budget (kg) [ ]

- Materials purchases budget (£) [ ]

- Labour usage budget (hours) [ ]

- Labour cost budget (£) [ ]

- The cost saving arising from the change in inventory levels for quarter 1 is

  £ [ ]

....

Task 4.15

The following sales forecasts are for periods of 20 days (four five-day weeks).

Sales forecast

	Sales forecast				
Period number	1	2	3	4	5
Number of Gammas	19,400	21,340	23,280	22,310	22,310

- On completion of production, 3% of units are found to be faulty and have to be scrapped with nil scrap value.

- Opening inventory: period 1

  - Finished inventory 3,880 units

  - Raw materials 16,500 litres

- Closing inventory at the end of each period

  - Finished inventory must equal 4 days' sales volume in the next period.

  - Raw materials must equal 5 days' gross production in the next period.

- Each unit requires three litres of material costing £8 per litre.

- Each unit requires 0.5 hours of labour.

- There are 70 production workers who each work a 40 hour week, for which each employee is paid a guaranteed wage of £240 per week.

- The cost of any overtime is £9 per hour.

Prepare the following budgets for Periods 1 to 3 and the gross production budget for Period 4.

	Period 1	Period 2	Period 3	Period 4
(i) Gross production budget (units)				
(ii) Materials purchases budget (litres)				
(iii) Materials purchases budget (£)				
(iv) Labour budget (hours)				
(v) Labour budget (£)				

Task 4.16

Extracts of the sales and production budgets of a product for the next four quarters are:

	Quarter 1	Quarter 2	Quarter 3	Quarter 4
Production (units)	3,100	3,600	4,100	4,500
Labour usage (hours)	9,300	10,800	12,300	13,500
Sales volume (units)	2,910	3,395	3,880	4,365

Assume there are 12 weeks in a quarter.

The production director is not happy with the production budget because there are only 29 production workers available, paid for a 35 hour week, and overtime is not possible. It is however possible to increase closing inventory, although this should be kept to a minimum.

The sales director is not happy with the sales forecast, and based on data from the past six years, has proposed the use of linear regression to help forecast sales, using the formula:

$$y = 1,000 + 100x$$

where y is the forecast sales trend measured in units of product, 1,000 is a constant and x is the quarter number. The relevant value of x for quarter 1 would be 25.

The sales director has also calculated the following seasonal variations based on the 24 observations:

Seasonal variations				
	Quarter 1	Quarter 2	Quarter 3	Quarter 4
Seasonal variation (units)	(500)	(300)	300	500

Produce a revised labour hours budget and hence production schedule, which removes the need for overtime, and complete the revised sales forecast based on the linear regression equation.

	Quarter 1	Quarter 2	Quarter 3	Quarter 4
Surplus/(shortage) in current labour budget (hours)				
Revised labour (hours)				
Revised production (units)				
Revised sales forecast (units)				

Task 4.17

A company manufactures and sells a single product X. The directors of the company are considering a new low price strategy for the year to 31 December 20X1 which would involve decreasing the price of X by 10%. This is expected to increase volumes by 15%.

The directors had already drawn up a draft operating budget based on their current pricing strategy and wish to revise this budget to see what might happen if the new strategy was adopted.

(a) **You are asked to prepare a revised operating budget in the Revision column below and calculate the increase or decrease in profit that would result.**

Draft operating budget	Draft	Revision
Sales units	210,000	
	£	£
Sales price	7.00	
Sales revenue	1,470,000	
Variable production costs	924,000	
Fixed production costs	325,000	
Gross profit	221,000	
	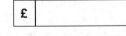	

Picklist

Gross profit will increase by

Gross profit will decrease by

(b) The draft budget for raw materials needed to make product X shows a figure of £427,500. This assumed a 5% decrease in production volume and the same raw material prices as last year.

In actual fact, new information now suggests that production volumes will stay the same but raw materials prices will fall by 10%.

Calculate the material cost forecast:

£ [   ]

(c) The draft administration salary budget is £244,800. This originally included the assumption that the annual standard 2% pay rise would apply from 1 January 20X1. However, due to the poor economic outlook the company has decided to decrease wages by 2% instead.

Calculate the revised salary budget:

£ [   ]

BPP
LEARNING MEDIA

Chapter 5 Preparing cash budgets

Task 5.1

A business makes 30% of its monthly sales for cash with the remainder being sold on credit. On average 40% of the total sales are received in the month following the sale and the remainder in the second month after the sale. Budgeted sales figures are estimated to be as follows:

	£
August	240,000
September	265,000
October	280,000
November	250,000
December	220,000

Complete the following:

	October	November	December
Budgeted cash receipts from sales (£)			

Task 5.2

A business purchases all of its goods on credit from suppliers. 20% of purchases are offered a discount of 2% for payment in the month of purchase and the business takes advantage of these discounts. A further 45% of purchases are paid for in the month after the purchase and the remainder two months after the purchase. Purchases figures are estimated to be as follows:

	£
August	180,000
September	165,000
October	190,000
November	200,000
December	220,000

Complete the following:

	October	November	December
Budgeted cash payments for purchases (£)			

Task 5.3

A business sells its single product for £50 which produces a gross profit margin of 40%. The product is purchased in the month of sale and is paid for in the month following the purchase.

Estimated sales quantities are as follows.

	Units
July	5,000
August	5,200
September	5,500
October	5,750

Complete the following:

	August	September	October
Cash payments to suppliers (£)			

. . . .

Task 5.4

Assume no opening and closing inventory.

Forecast annual sales of £6,000 and a mark up of 33⅓%, means forecast purchases of

£ [   ]

Forecast annual purchases of £12,000 and a margin of 20%, means forecast sales of

£ [   ]

Forecast annual sales of £16,000 and forecast annual profits of £6,000, mean forecast mark-up of [   ] % and margin of [   ] %.

. . . .

Task 5.5

A business makes all of its sales on credit with a 3% settlement discount offered for payment within the month of the sale. 25% of sales take up this settlement discount and 70% of sales are paid in the following month. The remainder are irrecoverable debts.

Budgeted sales figures are as follows.

	£
March	650,000
April	600,000
May	580,000
June	550,000

Complete the following:

	April	May	June
Budgeted cash receipts for sales (£)			

· ·

Task 5.6

A business manufactures and sells a single product, each unit of which requires 20 minutes of labour. The wage rate is £8.40 per hour. The sales of the product are anticipated to be:

	April	May	June	July
Sales units	7,200	7,050	6,550	6,150

The product is produced one month prior to sale and wages are paid in the month of production. Inventory levels of finished goods are to remain at 1,000 units until the end of May when they will be reduced to 900 units and reduced further to 750 units at the end of June.

Complete the following:

	April	May	June
Budgeted cash wages payments (£)			

· ·

Task 5.7

Recent actual and estimated sales figures are as follows.

	£
April (actual)	420,000
May (actual)	400,000
June (estimate)	480,000
July (estimate)	500,000
August (estimate)	520,000
September (estimate)	510,000

All sales are on credit and the payment pattern is as follows.

20% pay in the month of sale after taking a 4% settlement discount

40% pay in the month following the sale

25% pay two months after the month of sale

12% pay three months after the month of sale

There are expected to be 3% irrecoverable debts.

The purchases of the business are all on credit and it is estimated that the following purchases will be made.

	£
May	250,000
June	240,000
July	280,000
August	300,000
September	310,000

40% of purchases are paid for in the month after the purchase has been made and the remainder are paid for two months after the month of purchase.

Wages are expected to be £60,000 each month and are paid in the month in which they are incurred. General overheads are anticipated to be a monthly £50,000 for June and July increasing to £55,000 thereafter. 75% of the general overheads are paid in the month in which they are incurred and the remainder in the following month. The general overheads figure includes a depreciation charge of £6,000 each month.

Selling expenses are expected to be 10% of the monthly sales value and are paid for in the month following the sale.

The business has planned to purchase new equipment for £42,000 in August and in the same month to dispose of old equipment with estimated sales proceeds of £7,500.

Overdraft interest is charged at 1% per month based on the overdraft balance at the start of the month. At 1 July it is anticipated that the business will have an overdraft of £82,000.

Complete the cash budget for July, August and September.

	July	August	September
	£	£	£
Opening balance	(82,000)		
Cash receipts:			
Sales			
Proceeds from sale of equipment			
Total receipts			
Cash payments:			
Purchases			
Wages			
Overheads			
Selling expenses			
Equipment			
Overdraft interest			
Total payments			
Closing balance			

Task 5.8

An organisation operates in a highly seasonal sector of the retail industry. The company's management is estimating its cash requirements for the third quarter of the year, for which the following schedule of anticipated inflows and outflows has been produced by the sales and purchases departments.

Month	Sales	Purchases
	£	£
May	160,000	240,000
June	320,000	60,000
July	80,000	40,000
August	80,000	120,000
September	160,000	180,000
October	220,000	120,000
November	180,000	80,000

Sales are made on two months' credit, whilst suppliers allow one month's credit. Monthly salaries amount to £36,000 and the company's annual rent of £48,000 is paid quarterly in advance.

An overdraft of £112,000 is expected to exist on 30 June.

Complete the cash budget for July, August and September.

	July	August	September
	£'000	£'000	£'000
Opening balance	(112)		
Cash receipts:			
Sales			
Cash payments:			
Purchases			
Salaries			
Rent			
Total payments			
Closing balance			

Task 5.9

A manufacturing business is to prepare its cash budget for the three months ending 31 December. The business manufactures a single product which requires 3 kg of raw material per unit and 3 hours of labour per unit. Production takes place in the month of sale. The raw material cost is anticipated to be £9 per kg and the labour force are paid at a rate of £7.20 per hour. Each unit of the product sells for £75.

The forecast sales in units are as follows.

	August	September	October	November	December
Forecast sales – units	5,000	5,100	5,400	5,800	6,000

Sales are on credit with 40% of receivables paying the month after sale and the remainder two months after the sale.

Inventory of completed units is anticipated to be 500 until the start of October but this is to be increased by 100 units each month at the end of October, November and December.

The raw materials required for production are purchased in the month prior to production and 60% are paid for in the following month and the remainder two months after purchase. The anticipated inventory of raw materials is 3,000 kgs until the end of September and the planned inventory levels at the end of each month thereafter are as follows:

October	3,200 kgs
November	3,500 kgs
December	4,000 kgs

Wages are paid in the month in which they are incurred.

Production overheads are expected to be £60,000 each month and are paid for in the month in which they are incurred. This figure includes depreciation of £10,000 per month for machinery. General overheads are anticipated to be £72,000 each month in October and November increasing to £80,000 in December and are paid in the month in which they are incurred. The figure for general overheads includes £12,000 of depreciation each month.

The cash balance at 1 October is expected to be £40,000 in credit.

Complete the cash budget for October, November and December.

	October	November	December
	£	£	£
Opening balance	40,000		
Cash receipts:			
Sales			
Cash payments:			
Purchases			
Wages			
Production overheads			
General overheads			
Total payments			
Net cash flow for the month			
Closing balance			

Task 5.10

A manufacturing business has the following extracts from its budgeted statement of financial position and its budgeted income statement for the following year 20X5, along with the actual balances and results for 20X4.

Statement of financial position

	As at 31 December 20X4 £	As at 31 December 20X5 £
Receivables	23,000	19,000
Payables	5,600	12,800

The payables relate only to supplies of materials.

Income statement

	Y/e 31 December 20X4 £	Y/e 31 December 20X5 £
Sales	240,300	228,400
Materials purchases	120,000	128,000

Calculate the cash flows in respect of sales

£

Calculate the cash flows in respect of purchases

£

Chapter 6 Budget preparation – limiting factors

Task 6.1

A business has budgeted sales demand of 12,000 units in the coming month.

Each unit requires 2kg of material.

Each unit requires 0.5 machine hours.

Each unit requires 1.5 labour hours.

The availability of resource for the coming period is as follows:

Raw material available = 25,000 kg

There are five machines each capable of operating for 1,000 hours

There are 40 workers each capable of operating for 500 hours

No inventory of finished goods or raw materials is kept.

What is the limiting factor in the budget?

Select from:

- Sales demand
- Material
- Machine hours
- Labour hours

Task 6.2

A business makes a single product, each unit of which requires 5 kgs of raw material. Unfortunately, due to a shortage of suppliers of the raw material, only 129,000 kgs will be available in the coming year. The materials are available on a monthly basis spread evenly over the year.

Complete the following:

The number of units that can be produced in total is [   ]

The number of units that can be produced each month is [   ]

Task 6.3

The raw materials requirements for production for the next six months for a business are as follows:

	July	Aug	Sept	Oct	Nov	Dec
Raw materials requirements – kg	4,800	4,300	4,100	4,900	4,200	5,000

It is only possible to purchase 4,500 kg of the product each month.

Complete the following to show the maximum shortage of raw materials in kgs over the six-month period, monthly and in total, if only the amount required (up to the maximum allowed) is purchased each month.

Purchasing plan 1:

	July	Aug	Sept	Oct	Nov	Dec
Requirement						
Purchase						
Shortage						

Total shortage: [   ] **kgs**

Complete the following to show how many kgs of the material should be purchased each month in order to maximise production and keep inventory levels to the minimum possible. Give the total shortage of raw materials over the six-month period under this policy.

Purchasing plan 2:

	July	Aug	Sept	Oct	Nov	Dec
Requirement						
Purchase						
Excess/(Shortage)						
Inventory						
Production						

Total shortage: [   ] **kgs**

Task 6.4

Explain how a business could try to alleviate the problem of shortage of materials if:

(a) **The shortage is a short-term problem and full supplies will be available after a few months; or**

(b) **The shortage is a long-term problem?**

Task 6.5

The raw materials requirements for production for Selby Electronics for the next six months are as follows:

	May	June	July	Aug	Sep	Oct
Raw materials requirements – kg	9,500	10,200	10,200	9,300	10,200	10,300

Selby is only able to purchase 10,000 kgs of the material in each month.

Complete the following which schedules the purchases in order to ensure the maximum production over the six-month period together with the minimum possible inventory level. Give the level of shortage under this purchasing plan.

Purchasing plan:

	May	June	July	Aug	Sep	Oct
Material requirement						
Potential shortage						
Purchases						
Inventory						
Production						

Total shortage: [   ] **kgs**

Task 6.6

A product requires three hours of skilled labour per unit but there are only 12 such employees. They normally work a 38-hour week although, by paying an overtime rate of double time, it has been possible to negotiate for each employee to work eight hours of overtime a week.

The maximum level of production each week is [   ] **units**

Describe other ways of solving the labour shortage problem.

Task 6.7

Next week sales demand is expected to be 1,860 units. Each unit requires four hours of direct labour time and there are 160 employees each working a 35-hour week.

What is the overtime (in hours) required in order to meet demand with the current workforce?

Select from:

- 1,840
- 3,740
- 7,440
- 5,600

Task 6.8

There are two identical production lines in a factory. The factory operates two seven-hour shifts each day for five days a week with the production lines working at full capacity. The production line is capable of producing 30 units of product per hour.

The maximum production for a week is [   ] **units**

State the options that should be considered if sales demand were to exceed the maximum production level.

Task 6.9

Give three examples of possible key budget factors for a manufacturing organisation other than sales demand.

....

Task 6.10

In each of the following situations, suggest what may be the key budget factor:

	Key budget factor
A private nursing home with 140 beds. The home is situated in an area which has a large proportion of retired people amongst the population and there is little difficulty in recruiting suitable staff.	
A vendor of ice cream in a busy shopping centre. The transportable stall can store a maximum of 50 litres of ice cream.	
A partnership of three skilled craftsmen making carved chess sets from wood and marble for home sales and exports to specific order. Sales demand is high and orders have to be frequently rejected.	
A manufacturer of CD players and sound systems which are similar to those of other manufacturers and who distributes the systems amongst a number of small high street electrical retailers.	

....

Task 6.11

Four products have the following sales price and resource requirements.

	W	X	Y	Z
Sales price £	200	90	180	150
Materials (kg)	20	8	19	12
Labour (hours)	4	5	12	6
Maximum demand	300	1500	400	1000

The material costs £3 per kg.

Cost of labour is £6 per hour.

Materials are restricted to 20,000 kg.

Complete the production schedule.

	Production units
Product W	
Product X	
Product Y	
Product Z	

Chapter 7 Flexed budgets and variances

Task 7.1

The budget for production supervisors' costs for a period at an activity level of 250,000 units is £15,000. One production supervisor is required for every 100,000 units of production.

If actual production is 330,000 units, what figure would appear in the flexed budget for production supervisors' costs?

Select from:

- £60,000
- £20,000
- £15,000
- £19,800

Task 7.2

	100,000 units £	120,000 units £
Materials cost	240,000	288,000
Labour cost	124,000	144,000
Production overhead	38,000	38,000

The costs which would appear in a budget flexed to an actual activity level of 112,000 units would be:

Material cost

£ _____

Labour cost

£ _____

Production overhead

£ _____

Task 7.3

The budgeted production overhead for a business is £524,000 at an activity level of 60,000 units and £664,000 at an activity level of 80,000 units.

If the actual activity level is 72,000 units, the flexed budget figure for production overhead is

£	

Task 7.4

Complete the following flexed budget, given the following details of the cost behaviour of each of the costs.

Materials	the materials cost is totally variable
Labour	each operative can only produce 2,000 units each quarter – the cost of each operative is £3,500 each quarter
Production overhead	the production overhead is a totally fixed cost
General expenses	the general expenses are made up of a budgeted fixed cost of £6,400 and a variable element

Actual sales and production were in fact only 15,000 units during quarter 4. Prepare a flexed budget for an activity level of 15,000 units.

	Budget	Flexed budget
	20,000 units	15,000 units
	£	£
Sales (20,000 units)	130,000	
Material	(55,000)	
Labour	(35,000)	
Production overhead	(18,000)	
Gross profit	22,000	
General expenses	12,000	
Operating profit	10,000	

Task 7.5

Complete both the tables to show the variances of actual performance against budget, and then actual performance against flexed budget.

The materials and labour costs are variable costs, the production overhead is a fixed cost and the general expenses are a semi-variable cost with a fixed element of £13,600.

	Budget 28,000 units £	Actual 31,500 units £	Variances £
Sales	406,000	441,000	
Materials	165,200	180,400	
Labour	100,800	115,600	
Production overhead	37,500	39,000	_____
Gross profit	102,500	106,000	
General expenses	55,600	68,900	_____
Operating profit	46,900	37,100	_____

	Flexed budget 31,500 units £	Actual 31,500 units £	Variances £
Sales		441,000	
Materials		180,400	
Labour		115,600	
Production overhead	_____	39,000	_____
Gross profit		106,000	
General expenses	_____	68,900	_____
Operating profit	_____	37,100	_____

Comment on why there are differences between the variances shown in the two tables.

....

Task 7.6

Given below is the original fixed budget for a manufacturing operation for quarter 2. However, as sales and production were subsequently anticipated to be higher than this budget made allowance for, a revised budget was also prepared. The actual results for quarter 2 are also given.

	Original budget		Revised budget		Actual	
	200,000 units		240,000 units		230,000 units	
	£	£	£	£	£	£
Sales		1,360,000		1,632,000		1,532,000
Materials	690,000		828,000		783,200	
Labour	387,000		449,000		428,600	
Production						
Expenses	162,000		186,000		173,500	
Production cost		1,239,000		1,463,000		1,385,300
Gross profit		121,000		169,000		146,700
General						
Expenses		72,000		72,000		74,700
Operating profit		49,000		97,000		72,000

Complete the following flexed budget to reflect the actual level of activity for the quarter, and calculate the variances from that budget.

	Flexed budget units		Actual units		Variances
	£	£	£	£	£
Sales				1,532,000	
Materials			783,200		
Labour			428,600		
Production expenses	———		173,500		
Production cost		———		1,385,300	
Gross profit				146,700	
General expenses		———		74,700	
Operating profit		══		72,000	

Task 7.7

Given below is the budget for quarter 2 prepared using absorption costing principles. There was no opening inventory.

	Quarter 2 budget	
	£	£
Sales (50,000 units)		400,000
Materials	165,400	
Labour	69,800	
Production overhead	56,000	
Cost of production		
56,000 units	291,200	
Less: closing inventory	31,200	
Cost of sales		260,000
Gross profit		140,000
General expenses		52,000
Operating profit		88,000

The materials and labour costs are variable with the level of production but the production overhead and general expenses are both fixed costs.

Complete the following budget for quarter 2 using marginal costing principles, and reconcile the budgeted profit figure using absorption costing to the budgeted profit figure using marginal costing.

	£	£
Sales 50,000 units		
Materials		
Labour	_____	
Cost of production: 56,000 units		
Less: closing inventory	_____	
Cost of sales		_____
Contribution		
Production overhead		
General expenses		_____
Operating profit		======

	£
Profit per absorption costing budget	88,000
▼	
Profit per marginal costing budget	

Picklist

Production overhead included in closing inventory
Production overhead included in opening inventory
General expenses included in closing inventory

Task 7.8

A business's sales director unexpectedly resigns during the year.

What effect might this have on variances?

Task 7.9

Due to the sudden illness of the credit controller, the credit control function is outsourced to an external agency during the year.

What effect might this have on variances?

....

Task 7.10

Why is it important that managerial performance is only judged on the basis of controllable variances?

....

Task 7.11

Explain what is meant by feedback and feedforward.

....

Task 7.12

Given below is the original fixed budget and the actual results for the same period.

	Budget		Actual	
Units	*30,000*		*34,000*	
	£	£	£	£
Sales		660,000		697,000
Direct costs				
Materials	252,000		299,200	
Labour	180,000		192,600	
Factory power	83,600		88,600	
	515,600		580,400	
Fixed overheads	75,000		79,000	
Cost of sales		590,600		659,400
Operating profit		69,400		37,600

You are also provided with the following information:

(i) There is no inventory of finished goods

(ii) The production employees are paid per week irrespective of the production level. The employees that were budgeted for are capable of producing a maximum of 45,000 units in a six-month period

(iii) The budgeted and actual figures for factory power include a fixed cost element of £20,600

Prepare a report for the Chief Executive including the following:

A flexed operating statement for the actual activity level using marginal costing principles, calculating the variances for the sales and costs figures, as set out below.

An explanation of why the flexed budget operating statement shows different results from that of the original budget.

Units	Flexed budget 34,000		Actual 34,000		Variance A/F
	£	£	£	£	£
Sales					
Direct costs					
Materials					
Factory power	_____		_____		
Subtotal		_____		_____	
Contribution					
Labour					
Factory power					
Fixed overheads	_____		_____		
Fixed costs		_____		_____	
Operating profit		═════		═════	

Task 7.13

An original budget, revised budget and actual costs are shown for a period below, along with variances from the revised budget.

Budgeted and actual costs	Original budget	Revised budget	Actual results	Variances from revised budget
Production and sales (units)	24,000	20,000	22,000	2,000 (F)
	£	£	£	£
Variable costs				
Material	216,000	180,000	206,800	26,800 (A)
Labour	288,000	240,000	255,200	15,200 (A)
Semi-variable costs				
Heat, light and power	31,000	27,000	33,400	6,400 (A)
Fixed costs				
Rent, rates and depreciation	40,000	40,000	38,000	2,000 (F)
	575,000	487,000	533,400	46,400 (A)

Assumptions in the two budgets
1 No change in input prices
2 No change in the quantity of variable inputs per unit of product output

One invoice for heat, light and power for £7,520 had been incorrectly coded. The invoice should have been coded to materials.

Complete the following flexed budget and variances, after correcting for the miscoded invoice.

	Flexed budget	Actual	Variance A/F £
Production and sales units	22,000 units	22,000 units	
	£	£	
Variable costs:			
Material			
Labour			
Semi-variable costs:			
Heat, light, power			
Fixed costs:			
Rent, rates, depreciation			
Total costs			

The revised budget was set using a participative approach to budgeting, used to try to motivate staff.

Give two reasons why favourable cost variances may arise, other than due to better cost control.

Give two reasons why higher sales volume may not be the result of improved motivation due to the introduction of participative budgeting.

Task 7.14

A business makes a CD player that is fitted to the cars made by its parent company.

You have the following information.

- Two draft budgets for the coming year. The first assumes a production and sales volume of 80,000 CD players. The second assumes a production and sales volume of 100,000 CD players. Any differences between the two budgets arose entirely from the different volumes assumed.

- The actual operating results for the year.

- A note stating there was no opening or closing inventory of any sort.

- A note stating that there were no purchases or sales of non-current assets during the year.

The draft budgets and actual results from the working papers are shown below.

Budgets and actual results						
	Draft budgets				**Actual results**	
CD player production and sales volume	80,000		100,000		140,000	
	£'000	£'000	£'000	£'000	£'000	£'000
Conversion costs						
Labour	640		760		972	
Light, heat and power	370		450		586	
Rent, rates and insurance	200		200		200	
Depreciation	150		150		132	
		1,360		1,560		1,890
Bought-in materials		1,600		2,000		3,220
Total expense		2,960		3,560		5,110
Sales revenue		3,200		4,000		6,440
Operating profit		240		440		1,330

Complete the following flexed budget statement showing the budgeted and actual results and any variances.

	Flexed budget	Actual results	Variances A/F
Production and sales volume (CD players)	140,000	140,000	
	£'000	£'000	£'000
Conversion costs			
Labour		972	
Light, heat and power		586	
Rent, rates and insurance		200	
Depreciation	———	132	
Total conversion costs		1,890	
Bought-in materials	———	3,220	
Total expenses		5,110	
Sales revenue	———	6,440	
Operating profit	———	1,330	

The Chief Executive believes the high profits of £1,330,000 are due to increased effort by the managers following the introduction of performance related pay at the beginning of this year. Details of the scheme are:

- The bought-in materials for the CD players are purchased from outside suppliers but the conversion costs – those manufacturing costs that transform the raw materials into the finished product – are all provided the company.

- The only customer for the CD player is the parent company. Because of this, there is no market price and so the price has had to be negotiated.

- It was agreed that the price of the CD players sold to the parent company should be twice the cost of the bought-in materials.

- Additional performance related payments are based on the following.

    - Exceeding the annual budgeted volume of sales

    - Increasing the actual profit per CD player above the budgeted profit per CD player

- The budgeted sales volume for the year was 100,000 CD players and the budgeted profit per CD player was £4.40.

- The actual sales volume for the year was 140,000 and the actual profit per CD player was £9.50.

Write a memo to the Chief Executive, which covers the following:

Use the data in the question to explain THREE reasons why profits might have improved even without the introduction of performance related pay.

Identify THREE general conditions necessary for performance related pay to lead to improved performance.

Chapter 8 Performance indicators

Task 8.1

Suggest suitable non-financial performance indicators to compare budgeted versus actual performance for an online clothes shop.

....

Task 8.2

Suggest possible measures of productivity for each of the following types of organisation:

- A vet's surgery
- A bar
- A firm of solicitors
- A retail store
- A wedding-cake business

....

Task 8.3

A component is made by the manual operation of a number of cutting machines. The process produces shavings of material which are collected each day, and stored until removed by a rubbish collection service.

What performance measures or indicators will be useful to the production manager with regard to material?

....

Task 8.4

At an accountancy firm, trainees spend part of their time at college, and part in the office.

What performance measures will be useful for the Office Managing Partner in relation to trainees?

....

Task 8.5

A business uses a small number of large machines, which are only replaced every 20 years.

Suggest useful performance measures relating to the machines.

....

Task 8.6

Suggest performance indicators to measure customer service by a restaurant.

....

Task 8.7

A bus company collects the following information in order to monitor performance.

- Number of drivers
- Number of passengers
- Number of miles travelled
- Number of journeys undertaken
- Maintenance costs

This information is known over any time period.

Suggest measures that could be used to compare budgeted and actual performance in order to monitor the following performance indicators:

- Driver productivity
- Satisfaction of passenger needs indicators, using the information collected
- Satisfaction of passenger needs indicators, which would require other information
- Safety indicators, using existing information
- Safety indicators, requiring other information

....

Answer bank

Answer bank

Chapter 1

Task 1.1

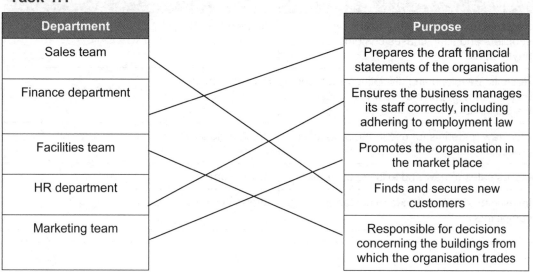

Department		Purpose
Sales team		Prepares the draft financial statements of the organisation
Finance department		Ensures the business manages its staff correctly, including adhering to employment law
Facilities team		Promotes the organisation in the market place
HR department		Finds and secures new customers
Marketing team		Responsible for decisions concerning the buildings from which the organisation trades

Task 1.2

Cost	Budget
Market research survey	Marketing budget
Wages of factory workers	Production budget
Recruitment advertisement for a new finance director in an accountancy magazine	Administrative overheads budget
Raw material costs	Production budget
Salary of marketing director	Marketing budget

Task 1.3

Function	Department
Prepares accounting information, pays suppliers and staff, chases customers for payment etc	Finance department
Recruits, develops and disciplines staff, and ensures that employment law is followed by the business	HR department
Buys raw materials for use in the production process	Purchasing team
Makes sales to new and existing customers	Sales team
Investigates and responds to customer complaints	After-sales service team

Task 1.4

Cost	Behaviour
Room hire	Fixed
Food for attendees	Variable
Hire of waiting staff – 1 required per 20 attendees	Stepped

Task 1.5

The correct answer is: True

Workings

	20,000 units	32,000 units
Total cost	£128,000	£204,800
Cost per unit	£6.40	£6.40

Therefore this is a variable cost as cost per unit is the same at each activity level.

Task 1.6

Cost	Behaviour
Heating	Floor area
Rental on storage unit for raw materials	Average inventory of raw materials
Canteen expenses	Number of staff employed
Depreciation of factory building	Floor area

Task 1.7

	Cost behaviour
Cost 1	Fixed
Cost 2	Stepped
Cost 3	Variable
Cost 4	Semi-variable

Task 1.8

Activity level (units)	Budgeted total production cost £	Budgeted cost per unit £
8,000	33,400	4.175
12,000	42,600	3.550
15,000	49,500	3.300

Workings

	8,000 units	12,000 units	15,000 units
	£	£	£
Variable costs			
£23,000/10,000 × 8,000	18,400		
£23,000/10,000 × 12,000		27,600	
£23,000/10,000 × 15,000			34,500
Fixed costs	15,000	15,000	15,000
	33,400	42,600	49,500
Cost per unit	£4.175	£3.55	£3.30

Task 1.9

	Cost behaviour
Maintenance contract which costs £10,000 annually plus an average of £500 cost per call out	Semi-variable
Sales car depreciation based on miles travelled	Variable
Machine consumables cost based on machine hours	Variable
Rent for a building that houses the factory, stores and maintenance departments	Fixed

Task 1.10

Costs	Accounting treatment
Servicing of office computer equipment	Allocate to administrative overheads
Materials wastage in production process	Direct cost
Depreciation of marketing director's car	Allocate to marketing overheads
Bonus for finance director	Allocate to administrative overheads
Sick pay for production workers	Charge to production in a labour hour overhead rate

Task 1.11

The correct answers are:

(i) Absorption costing

£	67.69

(ii) Marginal costing

£	61.46

Workings

(i) **Absorption costing**

Apportionment of overheads

	Cutting	Finishing	Stores
	£	£	£
Allocated overhead	380,000	280,000	120,000
Stores overhead apportioned 80:20	96,000	24,000	(120,000)
	476,000	304,000	–
Hours worked 50,000 × 3	150,000		
50,000 × 2		100,000	
Overhead absorption rate	476,000	304,000	
	150,000	100,000	
	= £3.17 per	= £3.04 per	
	labour hour	labour hour	

Unit cost – absorption costing

		£
Direct materials		16.00
Labour — cutting 3 hours × £7.50		22.50
finishing 2 hours × £6.80		13.60
Overheads — cutting 3 hours × £3.17		9.51
finishing 2 hours × £3.04		6.08
Unit cost		**67.69**

(ii) **Marginal costing**

Unit cost – marginal costing

		£
Direct materials		16.00
Labour — cutting 3 hours × £7.50		22.50
finishing 2 hours × £6.80		13.60
Cutting £380,000 × 60%/50,000		4.56
Finishing £280,000 × 60%/50,000		3.36
Stores £120,000 × 60%/50,000		1.44
Unit cost		**61.46**

....

Task 1.12

(a)

	£
Fixed production costs absorbed by the product	41,250
Over/under absorption of fixed product costs	3,750

Working

The fixed production overhead absorbed by the products would be 16,500 units produced × £2.50 (W2) = £41,250.

Budgeted annual fixed production overhead (W1) = £150,000

	£
Actual quarterly fixed production o/hd = budgeted quarterly prod'n o/hd (£150,000/4)	37,500
Production o/hd absorbed into production (see above)	41,250
Over absorption of fixed production o/hd	3,750

(b) **Profit for the quarter, using absorption costing**

	£	£
Sales (13,500 × £12) (W3)		162,000
Costs of production (no opening inventory)		
Value of inventory produced (16,500 × £8.50) (W2)	140,250	
Less value of closing inventory ((16,500 – 13,500) units × full production cost of £8.50) (W2)	(25,500)	
Total cost of production		(114,750)
Subtotal		47,250
Selling, distribution & admin costs		
Variable (13,500 × £1)(W1)	13,500	
Fixed (¼ of £90,000)(W1)	22,500	
Total selling, distribution & admin costs		(36,000)
Subtotal		11,250
Add **over-absorbed** production overhead (a)		3,750
Absorption costing profit		15,000

(c) **Profit statement using marginal costing**

	£	£
Sales		162,000
Variable costs of production (16,500 × £6) (W1)	99,000	
Less value of closing inventory (3,000 × £6) (W1)	(18,000)	
Variable cost of sales	81,000	
Variable selling, distribution & admin costs (13,500 × £1) (W1)	13,500	
Total variable costs (13,500 × £7)		(94,500)
Contribution (13,500 × £5)		67,500
Fixed costs: production (£150,000/4)	37,500	
selling, distribution & admin (£90,000/4)	22,500	
Total fixed costs		(60,000)
Marginal costing profit		7,500

Workings

(1)

	Production costs	Selling, dist & admin costs
Using Hi Lo method:	£	£
Total costs of 60,000 units (fixed plus variable)	510,000	150,000
Total costs of 36,000 units (fixed plus variable)	366,000	126,000
Difference = variable costs of 24,000 units	144,000	24,000
Variable costs per unit	£6	£1

	Production costs	Selling, dist & admin costs
	£	£
Total costs of 60,000 units	510,000	150,000
Variable costs of 60,000 units (× £6 or £1)	(360,000)	(60,000)
Fixed costs	150,000	90,000

(2)   The rate of absorption of fixed production overheads will therefore be:

$\dfrac{£150,000}{60,000}$ = £2.50 per unit

Total absorption costing production cost = £(6 + 2.50) = £8.50

(3)   Selling price: £432,000/36,000 units = £12 (or £720,000/60,000)

....

Task 1.13

File note

To: Drampton's finance director

From: Financial analyst

Date: xx/xx/xx

Subject: **Little Ltd – treatment of fixed overheads**

Following our recent discussions, I set out below calculations showing the reclassification of fixed overheads between the two units manufactured by Little Ltd, using activity-based costing.

	Allocated overheads to Server £	Allocated overheads to PC £
Set-up costs	10,000	-
Rent & power (production area)	24,000	96,000
Rent (stores area)	25,000	25,000
Salaries of store issue staff	8,000	32,000

Step 1. Calculation of cost per cost driver

	Budgeted total annual overheads £	Cost driver	Number of cost drivers	Cost per Cost driver £
Set-up costs	10,000	Number of set-ups	5	2,000.00
Rent and power (production area)	120,000	Number of wks' production	50	2,400.00
Rent (stores area)	50,000	Floor area of stores (m^2)	800	62.50
Salaries of store issue staff	40,000	No of issues of stock	10,000	4.00
	220,000			

Step 2. Reallocation of overheads based on costs per cost driver

Server	(i) Number of cost drivers	(ii) Cost per cost driver £	(i) × (ii) Allocated overheads
Set-up costs	5	2,000.00	10,000
Rent & power (production area)	10	2,400.00	24,000
Rent (stores area)	400	62.50	25,000
Salaries of store issue staff	2,000	4.00	8,000
			67,000

PC	(i) Number of cost drivers	(ii) Cost per cost driver £	(i) × (ii) Allocated overheads
Set-up costs	0	2,000.00	–
Rent and power (production area)	40	2,400.00	96,000
Rent (stores area)	400	62.50	25,000
Salaries of store issue staff	8,000	4.00	32,000
			153,000

Chapter 2

Task 2.1

A budget is a formalised, numerical plan of action for all areas of a business for the forthcoming period, normally set for the next twelve-month period.

A budgetary control system can help management to perform their duties in two main areas.

One of the roles of management is in terms of planning for the business – both long term strategic plans and shorter term operational plans. Budgets are formal, numerical plans which can help to ensure that all areas of the business are aiming at the same goals.

For example, once the sales and manufacturing budgets are set, management can then ensure that the budgets for other areas of the business such as the canteen and the sales department are in line with these budgets. So, for example, if it is budgeted that there will be 200 factory workers each day then the canteen should not be budgeting to buy food for 400. Or if sales are expected to be 60,000 units in the period it is important that the sales department budgets in order to be able to deal with this level.

A further important role of management is that of control of operations and of costs in particular. A budgetary system can assist in this area as the eventual actual results can be compared to the budgeted figures and any variances can be calculated and investigated. Where necessary management can then take corrective action to deal with these variances from planned costs.

Task 2.2

Scenario	Budget use
In order to meet a profit target, the managing director reduces the figure in next year's budget for the staff Christmas party by 25%	Control
The sales director divides the costs for client entertainment between his two sales teams, and gives the managers of those teams permission to spend within that level	Authorisation
A bonus cost of 2% of sales is included in the sales team's budget for the coming period	Motivation
A retail company is wishing to expand its operations and so includes the rental costs of new shops in its budget	Planning
The purchasing manager informs the production manager there will be a world-wide shortage of one type of material in the coming period. The production manager budgets for a different product mix because of this.	Co-ordination

Task 2.3

Strategic and operational plans

The strategic plans of a business are the long-term plans of the business. These plans will be based upon the strategic objectives of the management of the business which may concern maximisation of profitability, increase of market share, growth by acquisition of other businesses or expansion of the product range. Once the strategic objectives have been determined, then the strategic plans are the long term plans of how the business is to meet these objectives.

Once the strategic plan is in place then the management can look at shorter term plans necessary in order to meet the strategic objectives of the business. These are the operational plans and will take a variety of forms such as plans for the purchase of fixed assets, plans for the amount of production and plans for the financing of the business. All of these plans take the form of budgets.

Setting of strategic and operational plans

When a business is started the management must determine a long-term plan of how the business is to be operated and where its future lies. This will mean that the senior management of the business must determine the strategic objectives of the business.

The strategic plan will remain in place for the life of the business but may be altered from time to time as circumstances change or opportunities become available.

The strategic plan shows where the business is going but the next stage of the planning process is to determine how the business is going to get there. This will involve a detailed review of the business both from an internal and external perspective in order to decide what possible strategies there are in order to move the business closer to the strategic objective.

Information will need to be gathered about all of the resources of the business, the state of its products or services and the amount of finance that is available. External information about the market, competitors and the general economic environment will also be required. This detailed review of the position of the business is often called a SWOT analysis, a review of the strengths, weaknesses, opportunities and threats to the business.

Once this analysis has been carried out, management will be in a position to identify the various strategies that are available to the organisation, such as marketing a new product or concentrating on the production of its current products.

Once the various available strategies have been identified then the management will be in a position to choose which strategy is the most suitable and has the greatest potential for achieving the overall strategic objective. When the strategies for the future have been chosen then they can be co-ordinated into the strategic plan for the business.

Once the strategic plan is in place then the management can look at shorter term plans necessary in order to meet the strategies chosen for the business, the operational plans.

Tutorial note: this task (and many of the others in this chapter) has been included to help you learn about and understand the planning process in a business, but the answer is more detailed than any you would be expected to give in the assessment.

Task 2.4

Budget manual

The budget manual is a set of detailed instructions as to how the budget is to be prepared. The budget manual might typically include the following:

- The names of the budget holders – those responsible for producing each budget
- To whom each budget holder reports
- An organisation chart
- The timescale for the production of each budget
- The procedures for preparing each budget
- The format of the budgets
- How and when actual performance is compared to budget

Budget committee

The budget committee is responsible for co-ordinating and administering all of the individual budgets and will review and authorise each individual budget. The budget committee will normally be made up of senior executives and each function of the business should be represented on the budget committee in order to ensure that there is full communication between all areas of the business. The budget committee will normally be assisted by an accountant known as the budget officer.

Budget holders

Budget holders are the managers within a business that are responsible for preparing each resource budget. In most cases the budget holder should be the manager who will also be responsible for ensuring that the activities meet the budget.

Master budget

The master budget is the final overall budget for all areas of the business. It is normally set out in the form of a budgeted income statement, budgeted statement of financial position and cash flow budget.

Task 2.5

Budgeting process

The budgeting process starts with the setting of the budget (forecast) for the key budget factor. This will frequently be the sales budget although, if manufacturing resources are the key budget factor, this may be the labour budget or machine hours budget. Once the key budget factor budget has been set then the production budget will be set by the production manager and the various other resource budgets set by the relevant budget holders.

Once the budget holder has drafted his budget then he will submit this to the budget committee. The budget officer will ensure that the budget is consistent with the other resource budgets, checking, for example, that it has been prepared in line with the production budget.

There will then frequently be negotiations between the budget committee and the budget holder regarding the detailed content of the budget. The manager might for example have built in an increase in costs over previous years which the budget committee does not agree with. The budget holder may well have to change his draft budget and re-submit it to the budget committee a number of times before the budget committee is satisfied with it.

Once the budget committee have agreed all of the resource budgets with the budget holders then they will be formed into the master budget.

Task 2.6

Rolling budget

A rolling budget is one which is constantly being updated and added to. It will be set in detail for the next short accounting period and in outline for the remainder of the 12-month period. As each accounting period passes, the details of the next period's budget are produced and the budget extended to maintain a 12-month coverage.

For example if budgets are set for each of 13 four-week periods in a year, initially the detailed budget will be set for period 1 and the remaining 12 periods' budgets will be in outline. Towards the end of period 1 the detail for period 2's budget will be set and the outline budget for period 1 of the following year added.

The benefits of a rolling budget are that the detailed budgeting only has to be performed for the next accounting period rather than for periods a long time in advance, therefore the budget is potentially more accurate. This makes it more useful to you when assessing the performance of the business by comparing actual results with the budgeted figures. It also means that when setting the detail of each period's budget, the budget holder can react to changes in circumstances that are revealed by comparison of the actual figures for each period to the budgeted figures.

··

Task 2.7

To: Managing Director

From: An Accountant

Subject: The budgeting process

Date: XX XX XX

The method of budgeting that is usually used may not be the most appropriate for the business.

Current method

The current method is incremental budgeting, as this takes the prior year budget and adjust the costs included for changes in price and level of output.

However, the activities of the business, and how these are carried out, may have changed significantly over recent years. For example, the production process may now use more advanced machinery, and less labour, leading to higher power, maintenance and depreciation costs, but lower labour costs. This means the costs may be out of date.

The current method of budgeting does not encourage costs savings or efficiencies, as inefficiencies and any budget slack are rolled forward year-on-year. As various costs are never kept within budget, with no apparent consequences, there is no motivation to stick to the budget.

Zero-based budgeting

An alternative would be to use zero-based budgeting. This looks at the costs of each cost centre from scratch for each period. Each cost is considered in the context of the production budget and the amount of each cost must then be specifically justified and not just included in the budget because it was in last year's budget.

For each item of activity which causes a cost, the following types of question must be asked:

- Is the activity necessary?
- Are there alternatives to this activity?
- What are the costs of the alternative?
- What would happen if the activity were not carried out?
- Is the expense of the activity worth the benefit?

By asking such questions, the activity and its related costs can either be justified for inclusion in the budget or a cheaper alternative found.

Using this method would therefore promote cost-savings and efficiencies, eliminate budgetary slack and motivate staff as the budget is realistic, but challenging.

Chapter 3

Task 3.1

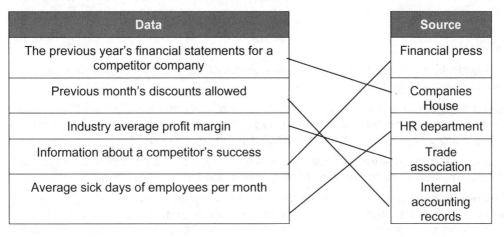

Data	Source
The previous year's financial statements for a competitor company	Financial press
Previous month's discounts allowed	Companies House
Industry average profit margin	HR department
Information about a competitor's success	Trade association
Average sick days of employees per month	Internal accounting records

Task 3.2

The correct answer is: Forecast production units and labour hours per unit

The labour usage budget requires the forecast production units and labour hours per unit.

Task 3.3

The correct answer is: Opening and closing inventory of raw materials.

If the materials usage budget is already known, this will have already taken account of inventory of finished goods, and the production budget.

Task 3.4

A capital budget details the timing and value of the purchases of non-current assets. This is important for a number of reasons.

- The purchase of non-current assets will normally be the most significant outgoing of a business and therefore it is important that such major purchases are properly planned.

- The purchase of non-current assets will normally be costly and it is therefore important that appropriate finance is available at the precise time that it is required.

- Non-current assets are frequently fundamental to the production and processes of an organisation therefore it is vital that non-current assets are fully functioning and are replaced or updated at the appropriate time.

Task 3.5

Resource budgets are those that deal with all aspects of the short term operations of the business. The resource budgets will include:

Production budget – this is a budget for the number of units that it is planned to produce during the forthcoming period – this will be based upon the key budget factor which is frequently the sales demand which will be forecast in the sales budget.

Materials usage budget – this is based upon the production budget and is a budget for the estimated quantity of materials that is to be used in the forthcoming period.

Materials purchases budget – this is the amount of raw materials that must be purchased each period to satisfy the production and inventory demands and will be expressed in both units and monetary amounts. These figures will be based upon the materials usage budget.

Labour usage budget – this is based upon the production budget and is an estimate of the labour hours required during the period to meet the production figures. The production budget will be the starting point for determining the labour usage budget.

Labour cost budget – this is based upon the labour usage budget and is the monetary cost of the labour hours required for the period, including any overtime.

Machine hours budget – this is based upon the production plans and shows the number of hours that the machinery must be working in order to produce the required level of production. The figures can be calculated using the quantity of production from the production budget.

Variable overheads budget – this will be based upon the production budget as the variable overheads will vary with the amount of production. Therefore the production budget will provide the quantities of production which can then be used to determine the variable overheads expected to be incurred.

Fixed overheads budget – this is independent of the level of production, as this should not affect the amount of fixed overheads. Therefore the budget for fixed overheads will be based upon estimates of fixed overhead costs and previous experience.

There may also be sundry other resource budgets such as the selling and distribution costs budget, advertising budget and the administration budget which will again all be set within the context of the sales budget.

Task 3.6

The general limitations of forecasting are:

- The less historical data that is used, the more unreliable the results of the forecast will be.

- The further into the future that the forecast considers, the more unreliable it will become.

- Forecast figures will often be based upon the assumption that current conditions will continue in the future. A trend of results may be based upon historical data, but you cannot always assume that the trend will continue in the future.

- If the forecast is based upon a trend, there are always random elements or variations which cause the trend to change.

- The forecast produced from the historical data may be quite accurate but the actual future results may be very different from the forecast figures due to changes in the political, economic or technological environment within which the business operates.

Task 3.7

Quarter	Forecast sales (units)
Quarter 2	112,060
Quarter 3	136,262
Quarter 4	118,611

Workings

	Trend	Seasonal variation		Forecast
Quarter 2 ((122,000 – 6,000) × 1.035)	120,060	– 8,000	=	112,060
Quarter 3 (120,060 × 1.035)	124,262	+12,000	=	136,262
Quarter 4 (124,262 × 1.035)	128,611	–10,000	=	118,611

Task 3.8

Quarter	Forecast sales (units)
Quarter 1	278,800
Quarter 2	417,450
Quarter 3	374,500
Quarter 4	319,500

Workings

	Trend	Seasonal variation			Forecast
Quarter 1 (Trend = 335,000 + 5,000)	340,000	×	0.82	=	278,800
Quarter 2	345,000	×	1.21	=	417,450
Quarter 3	350,000	×	1.07	=	374,500
Quarter 4	355,000	×	0.90	=	319,500

Task 3.9

The main limitations of using time series analysis for forecasting are:

- Unless the data used covers many years, it is impossible to isolate the cyclical changes due to general changes in the economy.

- The seasonal variations are an average of the seasonal variation for each period and again, unless this is based on a large amount of historical data, the figure could be misleading.

- Any random variations are ignored.

- The trend and the seasonal variations are assumed to continue in the future in the same manner as in the past.

- If the time series analysis is based upon historic values, the figures will include past inflation which may not be an indication of the future amounts.

Task 3.10

(a) The product life cycle is generally thought to split into five separate stages:

- Development
- Launch
- Growth
- Maturity
- Decline

During the development and launch stage of the product's life there are large outgoings in terms of development expenditure, non-current assets necessary for production, the building up of inventory levels and advertising and promotion expenses. It is likely that even after the launch sales will be quite low and the product will be making a loss at this stage.

If the launch of the product is successful then during the growth stage there will be fairly rapid increases in sales and a move to profitability as the costs of the earlier stages are covered. However, these sales increases are not likely to continue indefinitely.

In the maturity stage of the product, demand for the product will probably start to slow down and become more constant. In many cases this is the stage where the product is modified or improved in order to sustain demand and this may then see a small surge in sales.

At some point in a product's life, unless it is a consumable item such as chocolate bars, the product will reach the end of its sale life, which is known as the decline stage. The market will have bought enough of the product and sales will decline. This is the point where the business should consider no longer producing the product.

(b) If the future demand for a product is to be forecast using time series analysis it is obviously important that the stage in the product life cycle that has been reached is taken into account. For example, if the trend is based upon the growth stage, whereas in fact the product is moving into the maturity stage, then the trend would show an overly optimistic forecast for sales.

Task 3.11

The correct answer is: Maturity

During the maturity stage the pattern of sales is likely to be more constant.

Task 3.12

	Jan	Feb	Mar	Apr	May	Jun
Forecast variable production costs £ (production units × £10.50)	37,800	30,450	33,600	32,550	35,700	42,000
Forecast variable selling costs £ (sales units × £3.80)	13,300	11,400	11,400	12,160	13,300	14,440

Task 3.13

	Quarter 1	Quarter 2
Forecast direct materials costs £	667,396	722,633

Workings

Quarter 1	£657,000 × 128.4/126.4	=	£667,396
Quarter 2	£692,500 × 131.9/126.4	=	£722,633

Task 3.14

	Jan	Feb	Mar
Forecast variable production costs £	106,631	113,092	116,161
Forecast variable selling costs £	33,033	35,012	38,047

Working

Variable production costs

		£
January	4,200 × £25 × 137.3/135.2	106,631
February	4,400 × £25 × 139.0/135.2	113,092
March	4,500 × £25 × 139.6/135.2	116,161
Variable selling costs		
January	4,100 × £8 × 141.5/140.5	33,033
February	4,300 × £8 × 143.0/140.5	35,012
March	4,650 × £8 × 143.7/140.5	38,047

Task 3.15

The forecast total electricity, machinery maintenance and water costs for the coming month are

£	96,359

Working

		£
Electricity	£35,000 × 95% × 240.3/224.6	35,574
Maintenance costs	£20,000/4 × 2 × 1.05	10,500
Water costs	(£62,000 – 15,000) × 240.3/224.6	50,285
Total		96,359

Task 3.16

The forecast fixed costs for next year are

£	172,320

Working

		£
Rent	£65,000 × 1.055	68,575
Insurance	£15,700 × 1.10	17,270
Power	£84,000 × 171.2/166.3	86,475
		172,320

Task 3.17

The estimated variable cost per machine hour is

£	15

Working

	Machine hours	Cost £
June (lowest)	14,200	285,000
August (highest)	15,200	300,000
Increase	1,000	15,000

Variable cost = £15,000/1,000 hours
= £15 per hour

The estimated fixed costs of the maintenance department are

£	285,000

Working

	£
June	
Variable element £15 × 14,200 hours	213,000
Fixed element (bal fig)	72,000
Total cost	285,000

....

Task 3.18

Forecast units	Production costs £
74,000	685,000
90,000	797,000

Workings

	Activity level	Cost £
July (lowest)	63,000	608,000
September (highest)	76,000	699,000
Increase	13,000	91,000

Variable element = £91,000/13,000
= £7 per unit

BPP
LEARNING MEDIA

£

July

	£
Variable element £7 × 63,000 units	441,000
Fixed element (bal fig)	167,000
Total cost	608,000

Production level of 74,000 units:

	£
Variable cost £7 × 74,000	518,000
Fixed cost	167,000
Total cost	685,000

Production level of 90,000 units:

	£
Variable cost £7 × 90,000	630,000
Fixed cost	167,000
Total cost	797,000

The estimate for the 74,000 units of production is likely to be more accurate than the estimate for 90,000 units. Estimating the costs at 74,000 units is an example of interpolation, in that the estimate is being made for a production level that is within the range of production levels used to estimate the variable and fixed costs. 90,000 units of production is significantly higher than the levels of production used in estimating fixed and variable costs and therefore it is possible that the costs would behave differently at this level of production. This is an example of extrapolation.

··

Task 3.19

The correct answer is: a is the fixed element of cost, b is the variable amount per unit/hour

a = the fixed element of the cost

b = the variable amount per unit/hour

··

Task 3.20

The correct answer is: £810,000

Production costs = 138,000 + (6.4 × 105,000) = £810,000

Task 3.21

Power costs:

	Machine hours	Power costs £
April	80,000 + (380,000 × 0.5)	270,000
May	80,000 + (400,000 × 0.5)	280,000
June	80,000 + (395,000 × 0.5)	277,500
July	80,000 + (405,000 × 0.5)	282,500
August	80,000 + (410,000 × 0.5)	285,000
September	80,000 + (420,000 × 0.5)	290,000

Task 3.22

	Sales trend (units)
Month 1	25,600
Month 2	26,500
Month 3	27,400

Workings

Month 1: sales trend	=	3.1 + 0.9 × 25 (month 25)
	=	25,600 units
Month 2: sales trend	=	3.1 + 0.9 × 26
	=	26,500 units
Month 3: sales trend	=	3.1 + 0.9 × 27
	=	27,400 units

Task 3.23

	Sales volume
Quarter 1	1,590
Quarter 2	2,095
Quarter 3	2,125
Quarter 4	1,880

Workings

	Trend		*Seasonal variation*		*Estimate of sales*
Quarter 1	$400 + 105 \times 13$	=	$1,765 - 175$	=	1,590
Quarter 2	$400 + 105 \times 14$	=	$1,870 + 225$	=	2,095
Quarter 3	$400 + 105 \times 15$	=	$1,975 + 150$	=	2,125
Quarter 4	$400 + 105 \times 16$	=	$2,080 - 200$	=	1,880

Chapter 4

Task 4.1

The correct answer is: 13,200
Workings

	Units
Sales	13,800
Less opening inventory	(2,100)
Add closing inventory	1,500
Production	13,200

Task 4.2

The correct answer is: 189,500
Workings

	Units
Sales	200,000
Less opening inventory	(35,000)
Add closing inventory (70% × 35,000)	24,500
Production	189,500

Task 4.3

The correct answer is: 7,500 units
Workings

Opening inventory + production (P) – closing inventory = sales

$1,500 + P - 0 = 1.2 \times P$

$1,500 = 0.2 P$

$P = 7,500$

Task 4.4

The correct answer is: 16,702

Workings

Production required	=	16,200 × 100/97
	=	16,702 units

....

Task 4.5

	Period 1	Period 2	Period 3
Opening inventory	2,700	2,875	2,750
Production	10,975	11,375	11,050
Subtotal	13,675	14,250	13,800
Sales	10,800	11,500	11,000
Closing inventory	2,875	2,750	2,800

Working

	Period 1	Period 2	Period 3
	Units	Units	Units
Sales	10,800	11,500	11,000
Less opening inventory	(2,700)	(2,875)	(2,750)
Add closing inventory			
11,500 × 25%	2,875		
11,000 × 25%		2,750	
11,200 × 25%			2,800
Production units required	10,975	11,375	11,050

....

Task 4.6

	Period 1	Period 2	Period 3
Required units	12,000	11,000	12,500
Manufactured units	12,500	11,459	13,021

Working for example for period 1

12,000 × 100/96 = 12,500

If the answer is not a round number it must be rounded up to ensure sufficient units are produced.

....

Task 4.7

The correct answer is: 141,112 kg

Workings

Materials usage:

	Kg
25,400 × 5 kgs	127,000
Add wastage 127,000 × 10/90	14,112
Raw material required	141,112

Task 4.8

The material usage budget for the raw material is ▢ 200,000 ▢ kgs

The materials purchasing budget for the raw material is ▢ 194,000 ▢ kgs

Workings

Materials usage budget:

40,000 units × 5 kgs = 200,000 kgs

Materials purchases budget:

	Kg
Raw materials required	200,000
Less opening inventory	(30,000)
Add closing inventory	
(30,000 × 80%)	24,000
	194,000

Task 4.9

	Period 1
Materials usage budget in kg	320,000
Materials purchases budget in kg	343,500
Materials purchases budget in £	858,750

Workings (Period 1)

Materials usage budget:

	Kg
Production 32,000 × 8 kgs	256,000
Normal loss 256,000 × 20/80	64,000
Materials usage	320,000

Materials purchasing budget – units:

	Kg
Materials usage	320,000
Less opening inventory	(64,000)
Add closing inventory	
35,000 × 8kg × 100/80 × 25%	87,500
	343,500

Materials purchasing budget – value

	£
343,500 kg × £2.50	858,750

....

Task 4.10

The correct answer is: 400 hours

Working

One unit requires	18 × 100/90	=	20 hours
20 units require	20 × 20	=	400 hours

....

Task 4.11

The correct answer is: 400,000 hours

Working

Standard hours	120,000 × 4	=	480,000 hours
Actual hours	480,000 × 100/120	=	400,000 hours

....

Task 4.12

For quarter 1, the production budget is ⬚ 104,167 ⬚ units

For quarter 1, the labour usage budget is ⬚ 603,073 ⬚ hours

Workings

Production budget

	Units
Sales	102,000
Less opening inventory	(17,000)
Add closing inventory (115,000 × 10/60)	19,167
Production	104,167

Labour usage budget

	Hours
Standard hours 104,167 × 5.5	572,919
Actual hours 572,919 × 100/95	603,073

Task 4.13

	Period 1
Sales budget (£)	120,000
Production budget (units)	3,176
Materials usage budget (kg)	14,116
Materials purchasing budget (kg)	15,530
Labour budget (hours)	7,940
Labour budget (£)	63,520

Workings

	Period 1
	£
Sales budget (3,000 × £40)	120,000

Production budget	Units
Sales	3,000
Less opening inventory	(600)
Add closing inventory	
£3,400 × 20%	680
	3,080
Defective units	
£3,080 × 3/97 (rounded up)	96
	3,176

Materials usage budget	Kg
Production 3,176 × 4kg	12,704
Normal loss (× 10/90)	1,412
Materials usage	14,116

Materials purchasing budget	Kg
Materials usage	14,116
Less opening inventory	(4,200)
Add closing inventory	
16,040 × 35%	5,614
Purchases	15,530

Labour budget – hours	Hours
Standard hours	
Production 3,176 × 2	6,352
Idle time (hours x 20/80)	1,588
Total hours	7,940

Labour budget – £	£
7,940 × £8	63,520

Task 4.14

- The number of production days are $\boxed{60}$

- The closing finished inventory of Aye in units is $\boxed{125}$

- The closing finished inventory of Bee in units is $\boxed{200}$

- The labour hours available before overtime has to be paid are $\boxed{29,400}$

- Production budget (units): Aye $\boxed{1,495}$

  Bee $\boxed{2,359}$

- Materials purchases budget (kg) $\boxed{21,943}$

- Materials purchases budget (£) $\boxed{219,430}$

- Labour usage budget (hours) $\boxed{31,463}$

- Labour cost budget (£) $\boxed{259,956}$

- The cost saving arising from the change in inventory levels for quarter 1 is

  $\boxed{£ \quad 2,010}$

Workings

Production days	=	12 × 5	=	60 days

Closing inventory of finished goods:

Aye	=	1,500 × 5/60	=	125 units
Bee	=	2,400 × 5/60	=	200 units

Labour hours available before overtime

= 12 weeks × 35 hours × 70 employees

= 29,400 hours

Production budget

	Aye Units	Bee Units
Sales	1,500	2,400
Less opening inventory	(160)	(300)
Add closing inventory	125	200
	1,465	2,300
Faulty production		
1,465 × 2/98	30	
2,300 × 2.5/97.5		59
	1,495	2,359

Materials purchases

	Kg
1,495 × 4kg	5,980
2,359 × 7kg	16,513
Material usage	22,493
Less opening inventory	(2,800)
Add closing inventory (22,493 × 6/60)	2,250
Materials purchases	21,943
Materials purchases budget – 21,943 × £10	£219,430

Labour budget – hours

	Hours
Standard hours	
Aye 1,495 × 10 hours	14,950
Bee 2,359 × 7 hours	16,513
	31,463

Labour budget – value

	£
Standard rate: (35 × 12 × 70) = 29,400 hours × £8	235,200
Overtime: (31,463 – 29,400) = 2,063 hours × £8 × 1.5	24,756
	259,956

Cost savings:

	Opening inventory	Closing inventory	Reduction	Saving
				£
Aye	160	125	35 × £6 =	210
Bee	300	200	100 × £7 =	700
Raw materials	2,800	2,250	550 × £2 =	1,100
				2,010

Task 4.15

	Period 1	Period 2	Period 3	Period 4
(i) Gross production budget (units)	20,400	22,400	23,800	23,000
(ii) Materials purchases budget (litres)	61,500	68,250	70,800	
(iii) Materials purchases budget (£)	492,000	546,000	566,400	
(iv) Labour budget (hours)	10,200	11,200	11,900	
(v) Labour budget (£)	67,200	67,200	73,500	

(i) **Gross production budget**

	Period 1 Units		Period 2 Units		Period 3 Units		Period 4 Units
Sales		19,400		21,340		23,280	22,31
Closing stock (W1)	4,268		4,656		4,462	4,462	
Opening stock	3,880		4,268		4,656	4,462	
Increase/(decrease) in stock		388		388		(194)	
Good production		19,788		21,728		23,086	22,31
Faulty production (W2)		612		672		714	69
Gross production		20,400		22,400		23,800	23,0(

Workings

1   There are 20 days in each period.

Closing inventory = 4 days' sales in the next period = 4/20 of next period's sales

Closing inventory in period 1 = 4/20 × 21,340 =	4,268
Closing inventory in period 2 = 4/20 × 23,280 =	4,656
Closing inventory in period 3 = 4/20 × 22,310 =	4,462
Closing inventory in period 4 = 4/20 × 22,310 =	4,462

2   3% of gross production is scrapped. Good production therefore represents 97% (or 97/100) of gross production. Faulty production is 3% (or 3/100) of gross production and hence 3/97 of good production.

Faulty production is $3/97 \times$ good production.

(ii) **Materials purchases budget**

	Period 1 Litres	Period 2 Litres	Period 3 Litres
Material used in production (W1)	61,200	67,200	71,400
Closing inventory (W2)	16,800	17,850	17,250
Opening inventory	16,500	16,800	17,850
Increase/(decrease) in inventory	300	1,050	(600)
Purchases (litres)	61,500	68,250	70,800

Workings

1   Each unit requires three litres of material.

Material used in production = $3 \times$ gross production (calculated in (i) above)

Material used in production, period 1 = $3 \times 20,400$ =   61,200
Material used in production, period 2 = $3 \times 22,400$ =   67,200
Material used in production, period 3 = $3 \times 23,800$ =   71,400

2   •   There are 20 days in each period.

•   Closing inventory must equal five days' gross production in the next period.

•   Each unit requires three litres of material.

•   Closing inventory in period 1 = $5/20 \times 22,400$ (from (i) above) $\times 3 = 16,800$

Closing inventory in period 2 = $5/20 \times 23,800 \times 3 = 17,850$

Closing inventory in period 3 = $5/20 \times 23,000 \times 3 = 17,250$

(iii) **Cost of material purchases**

	Period 1	Period 2	Period 3
Material to be purchased (from (ii))	61,500 litres	68,250 litres	70,800 litres
Cost per litre	$\times$ £8	$\times$ £8	$\times$ £8
Cost of material purchases	£492,000	£546,000	£566,400

(iv) Labour budget

	Period 1	Period 2	Period 3
Gross production (units)			
(from (i))	20,400	22,400	23,800
Labour hrs required per unit	× 0.5	× 0.5	× 0.5
Labour hrs required	10,200	11,200	11,900

(v) Cost of labour budget

	Period 1	Period 2	Period 3
Labour hrs required	10,200	11,200	11,900
Basic labour hrs available *	11,200	11,200	11,200
Surplus hrs/(overtime hrs)	1,000	–	(700)

* 70 workers × 40 hrs per wk × 4 wks = 11,200

	Period 1 £	Period 2 £	Period 3 £
Labour cost per period			
(guaranteed) *	67,200	67,200	67,200
Cost of overtime (700 × £9)	–	–	6,300
Cost of labour	67,200	67,200	73,500

* 70 workers × £240 × 4 wks

●●●

Task 4.16

	Quarter 1	Quarter 2	Quarter 3	Quarter 4
Surplus/(shortage) in current labour budget (hours)	2,880	1,380	(120)	(1,320)
Revised labour (hours)	9,360	12,180	12,180	12,180
Revised production (units)	3,120	4,060	4,060	4,060
Revised sales forecast (units)	3,000	3,300	4,000	4,300

Workings

Surplus/(shortage) in current labour budget

	Quarter 1	Quarter 2	Quarter 3	Quarter 4
Labour hours required	9,300	10,800	12,300	13,500
Guaranteed hours (W)	12,180	12,180	12,180	12,180
Surplus hours/(overtime hours)	2,880	1,380	(120)	(1,320)

Guaranteed hours = 35 hours × 12 weeks × 29 workers

Revised budget of labour hours to reduce overtime

By rescheduling overtime as shown in the budget below, the total overtime hours can be reduced, with production being carried out within guaranteed hours in quarters 1 and 2, when there are surplus hours.

	Quarter 1	Quarter 2	Quarter 3	Quarter 4
Surplus hours/(overtime hours)	2,880	1,380	(120)	(1,320)
Original hours worked	9,300	10,800	12,300	13,500
Reschedule quarter 3's overtime		120	(120)	
Reschedule quarter 4's overtime	60	1,260		(1,320)
Revised labour hours	9,360	12,180	12,180	12,180

Revised production budget

A revised production budget which takes account of the rescheduling above is shown below.

	Quarter 1	Quarter 2	Quarter 3	Quarter 4
Revised labour hours (above)	9,360	12,180	12,180	12,180
Revised production budget (W)	3,120	4,060	4,060	4,060

Check: Total revised production = 15,300 units = original production (3,100 + 3,600 + 4,100 + 4,500)

Labour hours per unit = 9,300 hours/3,100 units (from original budget) = 3 hours per unit.

Forecast sales volume

Using the regression line y = 1,000 + 100x established by the sales director, the trend for quarters 1 to 4 can be established (with x in quarter 1 = 25).

Quarter 1:	1,000 + (100 × 25) = 3,500 units
Quarter 2:	1,000 + (100 × 26) = 3,600 units
Quarter 3:	1,000 + (100 × 27) = 3,700 units
Quarter 4:	1,000 + (100 × 28) = 3,800 units

The forecast sales volume is established by adjusting the trend values, set out above, by the seasonal variations, calculated by the sales director.

Quarter 1:	3,500 – 500 = 3,000 units
Quarter 2:	3,600 – 300 = 3,300 units
Quarter 3:	3,700 + 300 = 4,000 units
Quarter 4:	3,800 + 500 = 4,300 units

● ●

Task 4.17

(a)

Sales units (210,000 × 1.15)	210,000	241,500
	£	£
Sales price (7 × 0.9)	7.00	6.30
Sales revenue	1,470,000	1,521,450
Variable production costs (924,000 × 1.15)	924,000	1,062,600
Fixed production costs	325,000	325,000
Gross profit	221,000	133,850
Gross profit will decrease by		87,150

(c)   Revised material cost (£427,500/0.95 × 0.9)

£	405,000

(b)   Revised salary budget (£244,800/1.02 × 0.98)

£	235,200

● ●

Chapter 5

Task 5.1

	October	November	December
Budgeted cash receipts from sales (£)	262,000	266,500	250,000

Workings		October	November	December
		£	£	£
Cash sales	280,000 × 30%	84,000		
	250,000 × 30%		75,000	
	220,000 × 30%			66,000
Credit sales				
August	240,000 × 30%	72,000		
September	265,000 × 40%	106,000		
	265,000 × 30%		79,500	
October	280,000 × 40%		112,000	
	280,000 × 30%			84,000
November	250,000 × 40%			100,000
Total cash receipts		262,000	266,500	250,000

Task 5.2

	October	November	December
Budgeted cash payments for purchases (£)	174,490	182,450	199,620

Workings

		October £	November £	December £
August	180,000 × 35%	63,000		
September	165,000 × 45%	74,250		
	165,000 × 35%		57,750	
October	190,000 × 20% × 98%	37,240		
	190,000 × 45%		85,500	
	190,000 × 35%			66,500
November	200,000 × 20% × 98%		39,200	
	200,000 × 45%			90,000
December	220,000 × 20% × 98%			43,120
Total cash payments		174,490	182,450	199,620

Task 5.3

	August	September	October
Budgeted cash payments to suppliers (£)	150,000	156,000	165,000

Workings

	August £	September £	October £
July purchases 5,000 × £50 × 60%	150,000		
August purchases 5,200 × £50 × 60%		156,000	
September purchases 5,500 × £50 × 60%			165,000

Task 5.4

Assume no opening and closing inventory

Forecast annual sales of £6,000 and a mark up of 33⅓%, means forecast purchases of

£	4,500

Forecast annual purchases of £12,000 and a margin of 20%, means forecast sales of

£	15,000

Forecast annual sales of £16,000 and forecast annual profits of £6,000, mean forecast mark-up of 60 % and margin of 37.5 %

Workings

Tutorial note. In this question you are told that there is no opening and closing inventory, therefore purchases = cost of sales.

Remember **mark up** is on **purchases**.

If purchases 100%, mark up 33⅓,

Sales = 100 + 33⅓ = 133⅓%

$$\text{Purchases} = \frac{100}{133\frac{1}{3}} \times 6,000$$

$$= £4,500$$

Remember **margin** is on **sales**.

If sales 100% margin 20%

Purchases = 100 – 20 = 80%

$$\text{Sales} = \frac{100}{80} \times 12,000$$

$$= £15,000$$

$$\text{Mark up} = \frac{\text{Profits}}{\text{Purchases}}$$

$$= \frac{6,000}{16,000 - 6,000}$$

$$= 60\%$$

$$\text{Margin} = \frac{\text{Profits}}{\text{Sales}}$$

$$= \frac{6,000}{16,000}$$

$$= 37\frac{1}{2}\%$$

Task 5.5

	April	May	June
Budgeted cash receipts for sales (£)	600,500	560,650	539,375

Workings

		April	May	June
		£	£	£
March sales	650,000 × 70%	455,000		
April sales	600,000 × 25% × 97%	145,500		
	600,000 × 70%		420,000	
May sales	580,000 × 25% × 97%		140,650	
	580,000 × 70%			406,000
June sales	550,000 × 25% × 97%			133,375
Total cash receipts		600,500	560,650	539,375

Task 5.6

	April	May	June
Budgeted cash wages payments (£)	19,740	18,060	16,800

Workings

Production budget

	March	April	May	June
	Units	Units	Units	Units
Sales next month	7,200	7,050	6,550	6,150
Less opening inventory	(1,000)	(1,000)	(1,000)	(900)
Add closing inventory	1,000	1,000	900	750
Production in units	7,200	7,050	6,450	6,000

Labour budget hours

	April Hours	May Hours	June Hours
7,050/3	2,350		
6,450/3		2,150	
6,000/3			2,000

Labour budget – £

	April £	May £	June £
Hours × £8.40	19,740	18,060	16,800

Task 5.7

Cash budget – July to September

Opening balance	(82,000)	(42,420)	(23,254)
Cash receipts:			
Sales (W1)	438,400	467,840	488,520
Proceeds from sale of equipment	0	7,500	0
Total receipts	438,400	475,340	488,520
Cash payments:			
Purchases (W2)	246,000	256,000	288,000
Wages	60,000	60,000	60,000
Overheads (W3)	44,000	47,750	49,000
Selling expenses	48,000	50,000	52,000
Equipment	0	42,000	0
Overdraft interest	820	424	233
Total payments	398,820	456,174	449,233
Closing balance	(42,420)	(23,254)	16,033

Workings

(1) Receipts from credit sales

		July £	August £	September £
April sales	420,000 × 12%	50,400		
May sales	400,000 × 25%	100,000		
	400,000 × 12%		48,000	
June sales	480,000 × 40%	192,000		
	480,000 × 25%		120,000	
	480,000 × 12%			57,600
July sales	500,000 × 20% × 96%	96,000		
	500,000 × 40%		200,000	
	500,000 × 25%			125,000
August sales	520,000 × 20% × 96%		99,840	
	520,000 × 40%			208,000
September sales	510,000 × 20% × 96%			97,920
		438,400	467,840	488,520

(2) Payments to suppliers

		July £	August £	September £
May purchases	250,000 × 60%	150,000		
June purchases	240,000 × 40%	96,000		
	240,000 × 60%		144,000	
July purchases	280,000 × 40%		112,000	
	280,000 × 60%			168,000
August purchases	300,000 × 40%			120,000
		246,000	256,000	288,000

(3) **Overheads**

		July £	August £	September £
June overheads	$(50,000 - 6,000) \times 25\%$	11,000		
July overheads	$(50,000 - 6,000) \times 75\%$	33,000		
	$(50,000 - 6,000) \times 25\%$		11,000	
August overheads				
	$(55,000 - 6,000) \times 75\%$		36,750	
	$(55,000 - 6,000) \times 25\%$			12,250
September overheads				
	$(55,000 - 6,000) \times 75\%$			36,750
		44,000	47,750	49,000

Task 5.8

Tutorial note. Don't get caught out by putting all the rent in the budget.

Cash budget: July to September

Opening balance	(112)	(60)	184
Cash receipts:			
Sales	160	320	80
Cash payments:			
Purchases	60	40	120
Salaries	36	36	36
Rent (£48,000 ÷ 4)	12	–	–
Total payments	108	76	156
Closing balance	(60)	184	108

Task 5.9

Cash budget – October to December

Opening balance	40,000	45,020	43,020
Cash receipts:			
Sales (W1)	378,000	391,500	417,000
Cash payments:			
Purchases of raw materials (W2)	144,180	156,060	164,880
Wages (W3)	118,800	127,440	131,760
Production overheads	50,000	50,000	50,000
General overheads	60,000	60,000	68,000
Total payments	372,980	393,500	414,640
Closing balance	45,020	43,020	45,380

Workings

(1) **Receipts from credit sales**

	October £	November £	December £
August sales			
5,000 × £75 × 60%	225,000		
September sales			
5,100 × £75 × 40%	153,000		
5,100 × £75 × 60%		229,500	
October sales			
5,400 × £75 × 40%		162,000	
5,400 × £75 × 60%			243,000
November sales			
5,800 × £75 × 40%			174,000
	378,000	391,500	417,000

(2) **Purchases of raw materials**

Production budget

	Aug	Sept	Oct	Nov	Dec
	Units	**Units**	**Units**	**Units**	**Units**
Sales	5,000	5,100	5,400	5,800	6,000
Less opening inventory	(500)	(500)	(500)	(600)	(700)
Add closing inventory	500	500	600	700	800
Production	5,000	5,100	5,500	5,900	6,100

Purchases budget

	Aug	Sept	Oct	Nov
	Kg	**Kg**	**Kg**	**Kg**
Required for next month's production × 3kg	15,300	16,500	17,700	18,300
Less opening inventory	(3,000)	(3,000)	(3,000)	(3,200)
Add closing inventory	3,000	3,000	3,200	3,500
Purchases in kg	15,300	16,500	17,900	18,600
	£	£	£	£
Kg × £9	137,700	148,500	161,100	167,400

Payments to suppliers

	October £	November £	December £
August purchases			
137,700 × 40%	55,080		
September purchases			
148,500 × 60%	89,100		
148,500 × 40%		59,400	
October purchases			
161,100 × 60%		96,660	
161,100 × 40%			64,440
November purchases			
167,400 × 60%			100,440
Total payments to suppliers	144,180	156,060	164,880

(3) **Wages**

Labour budget – hours

	Oct	Nov	Dec
Production units (W2)	5,500	5,900	6,100
× 3 hours = labour usage (hours)	16,500	17,700	18,300
	£	£	£
Wages – production × £7.20	118,800	127,440	131,760

Task 5.10

The correct answers are:

Cash flows in respect of sales

| £ | 232,400 |

Cash flows in respect of purchases

| £ | 120,800 |

Workings

Cash inflows from sales = opening receivables + sales – closing receivables

= £23,000 + £228,400 – £19,000 = £232,400

Cash outflows on purchases = opening payables + purchases – closing payables

= £5,600 + £128,000 – £12,800 = £120,800

Chapter 6

Task 6.1

The correct answer is: Machine hours

The business can sell 12,000 units

The business has enough material to make 25,000/2 = 12,500 units

The business has enough machine hours (5 × 1,000 = 5,000 hours) to make 5,000/0.5 = 10,000 units

The business has enough labour hours (40 × 500 = 20,000 hours) to make 20,000/1.5 = 13,333 units

Therefore, the machine hours limit production to 10,000 units despite the sales demand being greater than this.

Task 6.2

The number of units that can be produced in total is $\boxed{25,800}$

The number of units that can be produced each month is $\boxed{2,150}$

Workings

Total production $=\ \dfrac{129,000\,\text{kgs}}{5\,\text{kgs}}$

$=\ 25,800$ units

Monthly production $=\ \dfrac{25,800}{12}$

$=\ 2,150$ units

Task 6.3

Purchasing plan 1

	July	Aug	Sept	Oct	Nov	Dec
Requirement	4,800	4,300	4,100	4,900	4,200	5,000
Purchase	4,500	4,300	4,100	4,500	4,200	4,500
Shortage	300	–	–	400	–	500

Total shortage   =   300 + 400 + 500

               = $\boxed{1{,}200}$ kgs

Purchasing plan 2

	July	Aug	Sept	Oct	Nov	Dec
Requirement	4,800	4,300	4,100	4,900	4,200	5,000
Purchase	4,500	4,500	4,500	4,500	4,500	4,500
Excess/(Shortage)	(300)	200	400	(400)	300	(500)
Inventory	–	200	600	200	500	–
Production	4,500	4,300	4,100	4,900	4,200	5,000

Total shortage: $\boxed{300}$ kgs

By purchasing the maximum available in August, September and November, even though it is not required, the shortages in October and December can be covered from materials held in inventory. This leaves only the 300 kg shortage in July.

....

Task 6.4

(a) If the shortage is only temporary then there are a number of short-term solutions which could alleviate the problem.

- Using inventory of materials – the inventory of raw materials could be run down in order to maintain production and sales.

- Using inventory of finished goods – in order to maintain sales in the short-term, finished goods inventory can be run down even though production levels are not as high as would be liked.

- Rescheduling purchases – if the amount of the raw material required is available in some periods but not in others, then the raw materials purchases could be rescheduled to ensure that the maximum use is made of the available materials.

(b) If the shortage is a long-term problem then the following are possible options for the business.

- Seeking an alternative supplier – this is an obvious solution but it may not always be possible to find another supplier who can supply the correct quality at an acceptable price.

- Finding an alternative material – in some instances a product can only be made from one particular material but it may be possible to adapt the design of the product and the manufacturing process in order to use a substitute material that is widely available.

- Manufacturing an alternative product – it may be possible to switch the production process to manufacture an alternative product which uses a different material which is not in short supply.

- Buying in finished goods for resale – instead of producing the product, it could be purchased in finished form from another producer who is not having the same problems with supply of the materials required. However this probably would lead to an under-utilisation of production resources and a major change in the organisation's strategy.

Task 6.5

Purchasing plan:

	May	June	July	Aug	Sept	Oct
Material requirement	9,500	10,200	10,200	9,300	10,200	10,300
Potential shortage	–	200	200	–	200	300

Do not buy 10,000 kgs each month as this will lead to inventory that is not required. However buy enough in May and August to cover the potential shortages.

	May	June	July	Aug	Sept	Oct
Material requirement	9,500	10,200	10,200	9,300	10,200	10,300
Purchases	9,900	10,000	10,000	9,800	10,000	10,000
Inventory	400	200	–	500	300	–
Production	9,500	10,200	10,200	9,300	10,200	10,300

Total shortage: | 0 | **kgs**

Task 6.6

The maximum level of production each week is | 184 | units

Working

Total hours available (including overtime)	=	$12 \times (38 + 8)$
	=	552 hours per week
Maximum production	=	552/3
	=	184 units

Possible solutions to this problem could be:

- Increase the overtime worked – it may be possible to agree additional overtime with the employees in order to maintain production; however at 46 hours per week already, this may not be an option here

- Use sub-contractors – in some types of business it may be possible to use agency workers or to sub-contract the work in order to maintain production levels. This option is likely to be fairly costly

- Use up finished goods inventory – if production levels are lower than required to meet sales demand, then for the short term sales can still be maintained by running down the finished goods inventory. This is not, however, a long-term solution

- Buying in finished goods inventory – this could be an expensive option leaving factory capacity under-utilised and may have quality implications as well

- Improving labour efficiency – this is not something that can be done quickly but with training over a period of time it may be possible to increase the number of employees with the skills required

Task 6.7

The correct answer is: 1,840

Working

Labour hours required	=	1,860 units × 4 hours
	=	7,440 hours
Labour hours available	=	160 employees × 35 hours
	=	5,600 hours
Overtime hours required	=	7,440 – 5,600
	=	1,840 hours

Task 6.8

The maximum production for a week is [4,200] units

Working

Hours of production line time	=	2 shifts × 7 hours × 5 days × 2 production lines
	=	140 hours
Maximum production	=	140 hours × 30 units
	=	4,200 units

If sales demand exceeds this maximum production level there are a number of options that could be considered.

- Introduce a third shift so that the production lines are in fact running for 21 hours a day.

- Lengthen the shift to, say, a 9 hour shift.

- Operate the factory for 6 or even 7 days a week.

- Speed up the production line so that more units are produced an hour.

Task 6.9

Any three of the following:

- Limitations on the amount of raw materials that can be purchased.

- Manpower limitations – a limit to the number of hours that can be worked in the period by the labour force.

- Capacity limitations – a limit to the number of machine hours available.

- A limit to the quantity that can be produced by a production line in the period.

Task 6.10

	Key budget factor
A private nursing home with 140 beds. The home is situated in an area which has a large proportion of retired people amongst the population and there is little difficulty in recruiting suitable staff.	Number of beds available
A vendor of ice cream in a busy shopping centre. The transportable stall can store a maximum of 50 litres of ice cream.	Quantity of ice cream that can be stored per day
A partnership of three skilled craftsmen making carved chess sets from wood and marble for home sales and exports to specific order. Sales demand is high and orders have to be frequently rejected.	Number of partner hours available
A manufacturer of CD players and sound systems which are similar to those of other manufacturers and who distributes the systems amongst a number of small high street electrical retailers.	Demand from retail stores

Reasoning

There would appear to be no limits regarding demand for beds or the labour force. The key budget factor would seem to be the number of beds available.

In a busy shopping centre demand for the ice cream is probably not the key factor therefore it is likely to be the quantity of ice cream that can be stored each day.

Sales demand is not a limiting factor however as this is highly skilled work the available hours of the three partners will be the key budget factor.

As the products are similar to those of other manufacturers and therefore can be replaced by similar products by the retail stores then it is highly likely that the demand from the retail stores will be the key budget factor.

Task 6.11

	Production units
Product W	300
Product X	250
Product Y	0
Product Z	1,000

Workings

	W (£)	X (£)	Y (£)	Z (£)
Sales price	200	90	180	150
Materials cost	(60)	(24)	(57)	(36)
Labour (hours)	(24)	(30)	(72)	(36)
Contribution	116	36	51	78

Kg/unit	20	8	19	12
Contribution/kg	£5.80	£4.50	£2.68	£6.50
Rank	2	3	4	1
Production	300	250	0	1,000
Kg used in production	6,000	2,000	0	12,000

Chapter 7

Task 7.1

The correct answer is: £20,000

£15,000 is the cost of 3 supervisors therefore each one costs £5,000 per period.

At a production level of 330,000 units four production supervisors will be required costing £20,000 for the period.

Task 7.2

Material cost (112,000 × £2.40) (W)

£	268,800

Labour cost (112,000 × £1) + £24,000 (W)

£	136,000

Production overhead (fixed)

£	38,000

Working

Materials	100,000 units	£2.40 per unit
	120,000 units	£2.40 per unit

Therefore a variable cost – £2.40 per unit

Labour	100,000 units	£1.24 per unit
	120,000 units	£1.20 per unit

Therefore a semi-variable cost

Variable element = £20,000/20,000 units
= £1 per unit

	£
At 100,000 units:	
Variable cost	100,000
Fixed cost (bal fig)	24,000
Total cost	124,000

Task 7.3

If the actual activity level is 72,000 units, the flexed budget figure for production overhead is

£	**608,000**

Working

Production overhead (72,000 × £7) + £104,000 = £608,000

$$\text{Variable element of cost} = \frac{£664,000 - 524,000}{20,000 \text{ units}} = £7 \text{ per unit}$$

	£
At 60,000 units:	
Variable element 60,000 × £7	420,000
Fixed element (bal fig)	104,000
Total cost	524,000

Task 7.4

	Budget	Flexed budget
	20,000 units	15,000 units
	£	£
Sales	130,000	97,500
Material	(55,000)	(41,250)
Labour (8 × £3,500)	(35,000)	(28,000)
Production overhead	(18,000)	(18,000)
Gross profit	22,000	10,250
General expenses (6,400 + 15,000 × £0.28)	12,000	10,600
Operating profit/(loss)	10,000	(350)

Task 7.5

	Budget	Actual	Variances
	28,000 units	31,500 units	
	£	£	£
Sales	406,000	441,000	35,000 (F)
Materials	165,200	180,400	15,200 (A)
Labour	100,800	115,600	14,800 (A)
Production overhead	37,500	39,000	1,500 (A)
Gross profit	102,500	106,000	3,500 (F)
General expenses	55,600	68,900	13,300 (A)
Operating profit	46,900	37,100	9,800 (A)

	Flexed budget	Actual	Variances
	31,500 units	31,500 units	
	£	£	£
Sales	456,750	441,000	15,750 (A)
Materials	185,850	180,400	5,450 (F)
Labour	113,400	115,600	2,200 (A)
Production overhead	37,500	39,000	1,500 (A)
Gross profit	120,000	106,000	14,000 (A)
General expenses (W)	60,850	68,900	8,050 (A)
Operating profit	59,150	37,100	22,050 (A)

Working

General expenses:

At 28,000 units – Variable element   =   £55,600 – 13,600/28,000
                                      =   £1.50 per unit

At 31,500 units:	£
Variable element 31,500 × £1.50	47,250
Fixed element	13,600
Total cost	60,850

Reason for difference in variances

The variances calculated when using the original fixed budget show favourable sales and gross profit variances and fairly large adverse cost variances culminating in an adverse net profit variance. However this is not comparing like with like since the original budget is for 28,000 units whereas the actual activity level is greater at 31,500 and therefore, in view of the higher activity level, both costs and revenues would be expected to be higher than originally budgeted.

When the actual results are compared to the flexed budget the variances are different. These variances reflect a truer picture since we are now comparing the actual costs and revenue for 31,500 units with a budget adjusted for the same level of activity.

There is an adverse sales variance and an adverse gross profit variance. The materials now show a favourable variance and the other variances are not so large. The final net profit variance however is much larger than the variance when compared to the fixed budget.

Task 7.6

	Flexed budget		Actual		Variances
	230,000 units		230,000 units		
	£	£	£	£	£
Sales		1,564,000		1,532,000	32,000 (A)
Materials	793,500		783,200		10,300 (F)
Labour	433,500		428,600		4,900 (F)
Production expenses	180,000		173,500		6,500 (F)
Production cost		1,407,000		1,385,300	
Gross profit		157,000		146,700	10,300 (A)
General expenses		72,000		74,700	2,700 (A)
Operating profit		85,000		72,000	13,000 (A)

Working

Sales – variable = £1,360,000/200,000 = £1,632,000/240,000 = £6.80 per unit

Materials – variable cost = £690,000/200,000 = £828,000/240,000 = £3.45 per unit

Labour – semi-variable cost

Variable element	=	$\dfrac{£449,000 - 387,000}{40,000}$
	=	£1.55
Fixed element	=	£387,000 – (200,000 × 1.55)
	=	£77,000
At 230,000	=	£77,000 + (230,000 × 1.55)
	=	£433,500

Production expenses – semi-variable cost

Variable element	=	$\dfrac{£186,000 - 162,000}{40,000}$
	=	£0.60 per unit
Fixed element	=	£162,000 – (200,000 × 0.60)
	=	£42,000
At 230,000	=	£42,000 + (230,000 × 0.60)
	=	£180,000

Task 7.7

Quarter 2 budget

	£	£
Sales 50,000 units		400,000
Materials	165,400	
Labour	69,800	
Cost of production: 56,000 units @ £4.20	235,200	
Less closing inventory	25,200	
Cost of sales		210,000
Contribution		190,000
Production overhead		56,000
General expenses		52,000
Operating profit		82,000

	£
Profit per absorption costing budget	88,000
Less production overhead included in closing inventory (6,000 × £1)	(6,000)
Profit per marginal costing budget	82,000

Task 7.8

The marketing or sales overhead variance may be favourable if the sales director is not immediately replaced, as the cost of the salary of the director is not incurred. However, if costs of recruitment are incurred, there may be an adverse administration or HR overhead variance.

There will be no effect on the sales variance, even if the volume sold decreases as the variance will be calculated after the budget has been flexed to actual activity levels.

Task 7.9

An adverse administrative overheads variance may be reported. This is because the administrative overheads will have increased as the salary of the credit controller would still have been paid while the external agency was also paid. The adverse variance may also be increased by the increase in irrecoverable debts if there was a break between the credit controller taking sick leave and the external agency being appointed.

Task 7.10

The importance of identifying controllable variances is in the area of motivation or de-motivation of management. If variances are reported, as part of the responsibility of a manager, over which he has no control, then this will have a de-motivational effect. If a manager is constantly held responsible for an adverse variance in a cost, the level of which he cannot influence, then this will not have a positive effect on the performance of this manager.

Investigating the causes of variances and determining any interdependence between the variances is an important aspect of management control because in a system of responsibility accounting the managers responsible for various elements of the business will be held accountable for the relevant variances. However they should only be held accountable for variances that are within their control.

There may be variances caused by factors which are beyond the manager's control, such as an increase in rent or business rates. There may also be variances in a manager's responsibility centre which have not been caused by his actions but by those of another responsibility centre manager.

An example is a favourable material price variance caused by purchasing a lower grade of material which leads directly to an adverse materials usage variance, as the lower grade of material means that there is greater wastage. The initial reaction might be to give credit to the purchasing manager for the favourable variance and to lay blame for the adverse usage variance on the production manager. However the true picture is that, in the absence of any further reasons for the variance then the responsibility for both variances lies with the purchasing manager.

Task 7.11

The process of continual comparison of actual results to budgeted results is known as feedback.

The budget period is normally for the forthcoming year; however, the feedback process should take place on a much more frequent basis. The calculation and reporting of variances should take place on a regular basis and will be daily, weekly or monthly depending upon the organisation. Any resulting action that must be taken in order to eliminate variances or improve efficiency should then be taken as soon as possible.

The information that is being received about the current performance of the business in terms of the current actual results can then also be used to influence the budget for future periods. This system of using information about the current performance for budgeting for the future is known as feedforward.

Task 7.12

Units	Flexed budget 34,000		Actual 34,000		Variance
	£	£	£	£	£
Sales (34,000 × £22) (W)		748,000		697,000	51,000 (A)
Direct costs					
Materials (34,000 × £8.40) (W)	285,600		299,200		13,600 (A)
Factory power (34,000 × £2.10) (W)	71,400		68,000		3,400 (F)
Subtotal		357,000		367,200	
Contribution		391,000		329,800	
Labour	180,000		192,600		12,600 (A)
Factory power	20,600		20,600		–
Fixed overheads	75,000		79,000		4,000 (A)
Fixed costs		275,600		292,200	
Operating profit		115,400		37,600	77,800 (A)

Workings

Budgeted unit selling price

$$= \frac{£660,000}{30,000}$$
$$= £22 \text{ per unit}$$

Budgeted unit material cost

$$= \frac{£252,000}{30,000}$$
$$= £8.40 \text{ per unit}$$

Marginal element of factory power
$$= £83,600 - £20,600$$
$$= £63,000$$

Budgeted marginal cost per unit	$= \dfrac{£63,000}{30,000}$
	$= £2.10$ per unit
Actual marginal cost	$= £88,600 - £20,600$
	$= £68,000$

Explanation of why the flexed budget operating statement shows different results from that of the original budget

The original budget was a fixed budget based upon the budgeted sales and production of 30,000 units. The flexed budget is based upon sales and production of 34,000 units therefore the anticipated increases in sales revenue and variable costs is built into this budget.

Task 7.13

Flexible budget comparison

	Flexed budget	Actual	Variance £
Production and sales units	22,000 units	22,000 units	
	£	£	
Variable costs:			
Material (22,000 × £9)	198,000	214,320	16,320 (A)
Labour (22,000 × £12)	264,000	255,200	8,800 (F)
Semi-variable costs:			
Heat, light, power – variable (22,000 × £1) Fixed element £7,000	29,000	25,880	3,120 (F)
Fixed costs:			
Rent, rates, depreciation	40,000	38,000	2,000 (F)
Total costs	531,000	533,400	2,400 (A)

Workings

	Original budget	Revised budget	Difference		Variable cost per unit
Production and sales units	24,000	20,000	4,000		
	£	£	£		£
Variable costs					
Material	216,000	180,000	36,000	(÷ 4,000)	9
Labour	288,000	240,000	48,000	(÷ 4,000)	12
Semi-variable costs					
Heat, light and power	31,000	27,000	4,000	(÷ 4,000)	1

Calculation of fixed costs and variable unit costs

The fixed element of heat, light and power costs can now be determined using figures from the original budget.

	£
Total costs	31,000
Variable cost (24,000 units × £1)	24,000
Therefore fixed costs of heat, light and power	7,000

Actual costs revised for miscoded invoice: Material = £206,800 + £7,520 = £214,320

Heat, light etc = £33,400 – £7,520 = £25,880

Two reasons why a favourable cost variance may have arisen

(1) **Managers may have included unrealistically high costs in the original budget**. This is a problem which can arise with participative budgeting; managers include extra cost allowances to ensure that they achieve their budgets. The submitted budgets therefore need careful checking, although this may be difficult because the managers themselves are the ones with the technical expertise.

(2) **Costs may have been lower than the level expected when the original budget was determined**. For example, an expected rise in rent or rates costs may not have occurred. Such savings are not necessarily the result of management control action.

Two reasons why higher sales volume may not be the result of improved motivation.

(1) The **market** for units may have **expanded** and the business could have reaped the benefit of a general increase in the demand for this product. This general market increase is not necessarily the result of improved motivation of sales staff.

(2) The sales staff may have **submitted an unrealistically low sales target** for the budget, to ensure that they achieve the target. Thus the fact that the sales volume is higher than budget may be a result of participative budgeting, but it may be due to manipulation of the system rather than improved motivation.

••

Task 7.14

Flexed budget statement

	Flexed budget	Actual results	Variances
Production and sales volume (CD players)	140,000	140,000	
	£'000	£'000	£'000
Conversion costs			
Labour (W1)	1,000	972	28 (F)
Light, heat and power (W2)	610	586	24 (F)
Rent, rates and insurance (W3)	200	200	–
Depreciation (W4)	150	132	18 (F)
Total conversion costs	1,960	1,890	70 (F)
Bought-in materials (W5)	2,800	3,220	420 (A)
Total expenses	4,760	5,110	350 (A)
Sales revenue (W6)	5,600	6,440	840 (F)
Operating profit	840	1,330	490 (F)

Workings

Budgeted selling price per CD player = revenue/sales volume

(£3,200,000/80,000 or £4,000,000/100,000)   £40.00

Budgeted bought-in material cost per CD player = bought-in materials/production volume (£1,600,000/80,000 or £2,000,000/100,000)   £20.00

Labour unit variable cost

Using the incremental approach:

	Volume		Cost
	100,000		£760,000
	80,000		£640,000
Incremental volume of	20,000	has an incremental cost of	£120,000

Therefore variable labour cost per unit = £120,000/20,000 = £6 per unit

Budgeted total labour fixed cost

	£
Total cost	760,000
Total variable cost (£6 × 100,000)	600,000
Fixed cost	160,000

An identical answer is possible by using the total cost for 80,000 CD players and deducting the total variable cost based on 80,000 CD players.

Budgeted variable cost of light, heat and power

Using the incremental approach:

	Volume		Cost
	100,000		£450,000
	80,000		£370,000
Incremental volume of	20,000	has an incremental cost of	£80,000

Therefore variable cost per unit = £80,000/20,000 = £4 per unit

Budgeted total light, heat and power fixed cost

	£
Total cost	450,000
Total variable cost (£4 × 100,000)	400,000
Fixed cost	50,000

An identical answer is possible by using the total cost for 80,000 CD players and deducting the total variable cost based on 80,000 CD players.

Workings for flexed budget

1 Variable cost of 140,000 CD players + labour fixed cost = (£6 × 140,000) + £160,000 = £1,000,000

2 Variable cost of 140,000 CD players + light, heat and power fixed cost = (£4 × 140,000) + £50,000 = £610,000

3 Fixed cost so the same at all levels of production

4 Fixed cost so the same at all levels of production

5 Cost of 140,000 CD players = £20 × 140,000 = £2,800,000

6 Sales revenue from 140,000 CD players = £40 × 140,000 = £5,600,000

MEMO

To: Chief Executive
From: Assistant management accountant
Date: xx.xx.xx
Subject: **Performance related pay**

Possible reasons for improved profit

The improved profitability may have occurred even without the introduction of performance related pay.

(1) The company cannot control the volume of sales as the only customer is the parent company. It therefore depends entirely on the level of demand from the parent company. This year they required 40,000 more CD players than budgeted and so, even without performance related pay, the sales volume target would have been exceeded. All other things being equal (ie no increase in fixed costs and variable costs per unit), this increase in demand would have increased profit.

(2) Part of the improved profit arose from an apparent change in accounting policy on depreciation. There were no non-current asset purchases or sales and hence the actual annual depreciation figure would have been known and should have been the same as the budgeted figure. The actual figure was less than the budgeted figure and so actual profit was greater than budgeted.

(3) The selling price per CD player is set at twice the cost of the bought-in materials. This means the more managers pay for the bought-in materials, the higher the price they can charge the parent company and so the higher the profit we can report. (Such a policy leads to inefficiencies, however, as managers are motivated to pay as much as possible for bought-in materials.)

(4) Fixed costs are the same irrespective of the level of production and sales. Hence the contribution will increase, all other things being equal, if actual volumes are greater than budgeted volumes and, with fixed costs remaining constant, so will profitability.

Note: You were required to provide only three reasons.

General conditions for improved performance

There are several conditions necessary if performance related pay is to lead to improved performance.

(1) Managers need to know the objectives of the organisation.

(2) Budgets must tie in with those objectives.

(3) Managers must feel that the objectives are achievable (although they should provide a challenge).

(4) Managers must want to achieve those objectives.

(5) Managers must be able to influence the achievement of the objectives.

(6) The level of rewards – both financial and non-financial – should motivate managers.

(7)   Managers must have the skills necessary to achieve the targets.

(8)   There should be a short period of time between effort and reward.

(9)   The actual results should not be capable of being manipulated.

Note: You were required to provide only three reasons.

••

Chapter 8

Task 8.1

Number of:

- Website hits per day
- Purchases per day
- Purchases per hit
- Customer accounts
- Returns per order

Task 8.2

- A vet's surgery — animals seen per day
- A bar — drinks served per employee
- A firm of solicitors — chargeable hours as a percentage of total hours
- A retail store — sales per employee
  — sales per square metre of shop floor
- A wedding cake business — number of cakes made per day
  — number of cakes decorated per day

Task 8.3

- Weight of shavings collected per day
- Cost of shavings collected per day.
- Weight of shavings collected per machine.
- Cost of storage of shavings before collection for scrap.
- Frequency/cost of rubbish collection service

Task 8.4

- Chargeable time of a trainee as a percentage of time spent in the office
- Cost of non-chargeable hours (because of training or lack of chargeable time in office)
- Cost of training per trainee
- Average time from joining firm to exam completion

Task 8.5

- Units produced per machine hour

- Total maintenance costs, and maintenance costs per machine

- Breakdowns (and so idle hours) per machine, or total lost machine hours per week/month

- Number of machines in operation per shift

....

Task 8.6

- Complaints per number of covers
- Time between order and meals being served

....

Task 8.7

Driver productivity

A possible measure of driver productivity is the number of miles per driver, or the number of journeys undertaken per driver.

Satisfaction of passenger needs indicators, using the information collected

The satisfaction of passenger needs could be monitored by the number of passengers per journey.

Depending on the size of the buses, passenger needs may be less satisfied if there are more passengers per journey because of more crowding or the need to stand because no seats were available.

Another measure of the satisfaction of passenger needs is the number of journeys per day, as this may mean reduced waiting times.

Satisfaction of passenger needs indicators, which would require other information

A measure of the satisfaction of customer needs that cannot be derived from the existing data is cleanliness of the buses.

Monitoring the cleaning cost per day or per bus might give some indication of the effort put into keeping the buses clean.

Another measure of the satisfaction of customer needs **is punctuality** of the buses and their **adherence to published** timetables.

Monitoring the percentage of buses arriving and departing within five minutes of their published time would give an indication of performance in this area.

Safety indicators, using existing information

The safety aspect of Travel Bus's operations could be monitored by the maintenance cost per mile, although a high cost may in fact indicate an older fleet, and so reduced safety.

Safety indicators, requiring other information

A measure of the safety aspect that cannot be derived from the existing data is the number of accidents per year.

Another measure could be the percentage of maintenance cost that is incurred to prevent faults compared with the percentage incurred to correct faults. This would indicate whether faults were being prevented before they occurred, or whether maintenance was being carried out 'after the event', which could compromise safety.

AAT AQ2013 SAMPLE ASSESSMENT 1
BUDGETING

Time allowed: 2 hours

Task 1 (16 marks)

(a) **Match each type of data with its appropriate source.**

Draw a line from a box in the left column to one in the right column to indicate each answer.

Type of data	Appropriate Source
	Financial Times
Competitors' prices	Trades Union
Competitors' wage rates	Trade Association
Prices index in the country in which we operate	Internet web site / browser
	Statistics published by Government (eg Office for National Statistics in UK)

(b) **As budget accountant, match each task with the person or group that you will need to contact.**

Draw a line from a box in the left column to one in the right column to indicate each answer.

Task	Contact
	Trade union representative
Agree planning assumptions for budget preparation	Production manager
Set budget pay rates	Human resources manager
Draft the direct labour hours budget	Marketing manager
	Budget committee

(c) **Write the correct answer from the left into its appropriate budget on the right.**

Sales force salaries	
Raw material usage	
Hire of delivery vehicles	
Payments to suppliers	
Cleaning materials for production line	
Replacement vehicles for sales staff	
Telecommunications charges	
Factory extension	

Capital expenditure

Marketing & distribution

Cash Flow

Cost of Production

Administration

(d) **Select the appropriate accounting treatment for each of the following costs.**

Cost	Accounting treatment
Repairs to sales office furniture	▼
Replacement of production machinery	▼
Raw material usage	▼
Product advertising	▼
Power for production	▼
Purchasing department	▼
Production labour – idle time	▼
Factory extension	▼

Drop-down list:

Allocate to marketing overheads
Charge to production in a machine hour overhead rate
Charge to production in a labour hour overhead rate
Direct cost
Activity based charge to products
Capitalise and depreciate over useful life

(e) **Select the appropriate term to match each of these descriptions.**

Description	Term
A cost that fluctuates in direct proportion to changes in activity	▼
Detailed budgets prepared by functional managers are collated to form a master budget	▼
Collecting data about a proportion of the items in the population to indicate the characteristics of the whole population	▼
A physical or financial measure to monitor efficiency, cost, quality, etc.	▼

Drop-down list:

Variable cost / Fixed cost / Semi-variable cost / Stepped cost

Bottom up budgeting / Top down budgeting / Rolling budgets / Zero base budgeting / Incremental budgeting / Budget flexing / Budget revision

Sampling / Census / Stratified sampling / Trend / Market research / Market analysis / Product life cycle

Performance indicator / Variance / Performance review / Variance analysis / Material cost variance / Labour cost variance

· ·

Task 2 (19 marks)

(a) **Complete the following production forecast for product Q based on the information below. Do not show decimals. Round any decimal figures up to the next whole number of units.**

Closing inventory should be 12.5% of the following week's sales volume. 15% of all production fails quality control checks and is rejected.

Production (units)	Week 1	Week 2	Week 3	Week 4	Week 5
Sales volume	400	450	500	600	550
Opening inventory	75				
Closing inventory					
Saleable production					
Rejected production					
Total manufactured units					

(b) **Calculate raw material requirements.**

Do not show decimals. Round any decimal figures up to the next whole number of litres.

800 items of product N are to be manufactured next week.

Each requires 14 litres of raw material.
8% of raw material is wasted during manufacture.
The opening inventory will be 700 litres.
The closing inventory will be 500 litres.

How many litres are required for production? [   ] litres

How many litres must be purchased? [   ] litres

(c) **Calculate Labour hours.**

Do not show decimals. Round any decimal figures <u>up to the next whole number</u> of hours.

65,000 items of product M are to be manufactured in May.
Each one takes 4 minutes to produce.
20 staff will each work 175 basic hours.

How many overtime hours must be worked to complete the production?
[   ] hours

(d) **Calculate sub-contracting requirements.**

Do not show decimals. Round any decimal figures up to the next whole number of units.

7,410 items of product X are to be manufactured next week.
Each one takes 3 minutes to produce.
350 production labour hours are available.
Any additional requirement must be sub-contracted.

How many units must be subcontracted? [   ] units

Task 3 (18 marks)

Operating budget

Enter the missing figures in the working schedules and operating budget using the data from the production budget and the notes below.

Production budget	Units
Opening inventory of finished goods	92,400
Production	589,000
Sub-total	681,400
Sales	600,000
Closing inventory of finished goods	81,400

(a) **Complete these three working schedules.**

Materials

Each unit produced requires 0.75kg of material. Closing inventory will be valued at the budgeted purchase price.

Materials	Kg	£
Opening inventory	50,000	60,000
Purchases	460,000	598,000
Sub-total	510,000	658,000
Used in production		
Closing inventory		

Labour

Each item takes 3 minutes to produce.

150 staff work 160 basic hours each in the period.

Overtime is paid at 50% above the basic hourly rate.

Labour	Hours	£
Basic time @ £16 per hour		
Overtime		
Total		

Overhead

Variable overhead is recovered on total labour hours.

Overhead	Hours	£
Variable @ £3.60 per hour		
Fixed		105,705
Total		

(b) **Now complete the operating budget.**

Enter income, costs and inventories as positive figures.

Closing finished goods inventory will be valued at the budgeted production cost per unit.

Use a negative figure to indicate a gross loss, for example –500 or (500).

Operating budget	Units	£ per unit	£
Sales revenue		2.35	
Cost of goods sold:			£
Opening inventory of finished goods			150,000
Cost of production		£	
Materials			
Labour			
Overhead			
Closing inventory of finished goods			
Cost of goods sold			
Gross profit			
Overheads		£	
Administration		61,200	
Marketing		49,800	

Use a negative figure to indicate a gross loss, for example –500 or (500).

Operating profit	

Task 4 (17 marks)

(a) **Stratified sampling**

Calculate the number of customers to be interviewed from each age group to obtain a representative response from 1,200 interviews.

Do not show decimals. Round to the nearest whole number.

Age range >>>	Up to 29	30 to 39	40 to 49	Over 49	Total
Number of customers	15,000	24,000	42,000	18,500	
Sample					

(b) **Break a budget down into accounting periods.**

Calculate the sales revenue and cost budgets for April using the budgeted unit data and the information below.

- Each unit is made from 3kg of material costing £0.75 per kg.

- It takes 5 minutes to make each item.

- 1,250 hours of basic time is available in the month. Any extra hours must be worked in overtime.

- The basic rate is £16 per hour. Overtime is paid at 50% above basic rate.

- Variable overhead relates to labour hours, including overtime.

- Fixed production overhead costs are spread evenly through the year.

Budgeted units	Year	April
Units sold	216,000	18,200
Units produced	210,000	18,000

Budget in £	Year	April
Sales revenue	1,166,400	
Material used	472,500	
Direct labour	300,000	
Variable production overhead	77,000	
Fixed production overhead	13,200	

(c) **Cash flow forecast**

Prepare the forecast from the operating budget and statement of financial position (balance sheet) assumptions. Enter receipts and payments as positive figures.

Statement of financial position (balance sheet) assumptions:

- Receivables will increase by £2,500.
- Materials payables will reduce by £3,500.
- Labour costs are paid in the period in which they are incurred.
- Other payables will increase by £4,800.

Operating Budget	£	£
Sales revenue		103,000
Expenditure		
Materials	34,200	
Labour	38,500	
Other costs	16,400	89,100
Operating Profit		13,900

Cash Flow Forecast	£	£
Sales revenue		
Expenditure		
Materials		
Labour		
Other costs		
Cash flow		

Show a net cash outflow as a negative, for example –500.

Task 5 (20 marks)

Budget submission

You have prepared a draft raw materials budget for the coming year

Background information

- The production budget (units) has already been agreed.
- The production manager and purchasing manager have decided to switch to a new supplier.
- The quality of the material will be improved which should reduce wastage.
- The material price will increase.
- Supply should be more reliable which means that inventory can be reduced.
- You have been asked to recommend performance indicators to monitor material costs and to give advice about ownership of the budget.

Draft raw materials budget	This Year Actual	Next Year Budget
Production (units)	64,000	67,840
Material per unit	0.4kg	0.4kg
Material loss (wastage)	12.5%	10%
Material	**kg**	**kg**
Required for production	29,258	30,152
Opening inventory	1,300	1,242
Closing inventory	1,242	1,000
Purchases	29,200	29,910
Material purchases	**£**	**£**
Price per kg	4.80	5.04
Purchases	**140,160**	**150,747**

Write an email to the budget committee, in 3 parts:

(a) **Requesting approval for the budget and explaining the assumptions upon which it is based.**

(b) **Suggesting 4 appropriate performance indicators (other than cost variances) to monitor raw material costs.**

(c) **Explaining which of the planning assumptions are based on forecasts and why these are not totally within the production manager's control.**

To: The Budget Committee   **From:**   Budget Accountant
Subject: Draft Raw Materials Budget   **Date:**   xxxxxx

(a) **Budget submission**

(b) **Performance indicators**

(c) **Forecasts**

Budget Accountant

Task 6 (18 marks)

(a) **Budget revision**

You have submitted a draft operating budget to the budget committee.

The committee has asked you to budget for an alternative scenario and calculate the increase or decrease in expected profit.

Complete the alternative scenario column in the operating budget table and calculate the increase or decrease in profit.

Assumptions in the first scenario

Material and labour costs are variable.
Depreciation is a stepped cost, increasing at every 10,000 units.
There is an allowance for an energy price rise of 4%.

Alternate scenario

Increase the selling price by 5%.
Reduce the sales volume by 10%.
Revise the energy price rise to 6%.

Apart from the sales price per unit, do not enter decimals.

Round to the nearest whole number, if necessary.

Operating Budget	First draft	Alternative Scenario
Sales price £ per unit	6.00	
Sales volume	84,000	
	£	£
Sales revenue	504,000	
Costs		
Material	201,600	
Labour	226,800	
Energy	17,680	
Depreciation	8,100	
Total	454,180	
Gross profit	49,820	
Increase/(decrease) in gross profit		

(b) **Variance analysis**

Prepare the direct labour cost statement from the activity data provided

Enter favourable variances as positive figures – for example 500.

Enter adverse variances as negative figures – for example –500.

Activity data	Items produced	Hours	Cost
Budget	18,000	288,000	1,728,000
Actual results	17,000	280,500	1,626,900

Direct Labour Cost Statement	£
Standard direct labour cost of production	
Variances (adverse shown as negative)	
Labour rate	
Labour efficiency	
Labour cost	

Task 7 (16 marks)

Operating report

You are required to complete the monthly operating report below. Flex the budget, calculate variances and show whether each variance is favourable or adverse. The original budget and actual results have been entered.

Notes

Material, labour and distribution costs are variable.

Energy cost is semi-variable. The fixed element is budgeted at £12,800 per month.

Equipment hire is a stepped cost, budgeted to increase at every 30,000 units of monthly production.

Depreciation, marketing and administration costs are fixed.

Monthly Operating Report

Original budget		Flexed budget	Actual	Variance Fav/(Adv)
178,000	Sales volume (units)		192,000	
£		£	£	£
1,281,600	Sales revenue		1,377,000	
	Costs			
462,800	Materials		500,100	
480,600	Labour		516,500	
67,640	Distribution		74,200	
60,860	Energy		65,080	
24,000	Equipment hire		28,600	
8,800	Depreciation		8,700	
78,000	Marketing		78,900	
25,600	Administration		24,820	
1,208,300	Total		1,296,900	
73,300	Operating profit/(Loss)		80,100	

Task 8 (15 marks)

Operational review

Review the operating statement shown and the additional information below, and prepare a report by email.

Additional information

The budget has been flexed to the actual number of units produced and sold. The original budget was based on an expected sales volume of 165,000 units which was expected to generate a profit of £227,000.

Sales volume reduced when a competitor undercut our prices. We responded with a 10% price reduction partway through the year and expected to win back most of the volume in due course.

The budget allowed for a significant amount of overtime working but this was not required when sales volume fell. Material usage efficiency was better than expected and a budgeted increase in material price did not occur.

The original budget was prepared by a management committee and approved by the Chief Executive. She is concerned that profit is lower than originally budgeted and asks you how she can encourage the management team to perform better.

Operating Statement	Flexed Budget	Actual	Variance Fav(Adv)
Sales volume	147,000 units		
	£'000	£'000	£'000
Sales revenue	**764**	**735**	**(29)**
Variable costs			
Material	221	212	9
Labour	125	110	15
Distribution	25	24	1
Power	9	9	–
Equipment hire	138	132	6
Total	518	487	31
Contribution	**246**	**248**	**2**
Fixed costs			
Power	15	14	1
Depreciation	16	17	(1)
Marketing	12	11	1
Administration	7	8	(1)
Total	50	50	–
Operating profit	**196**	**198**	**2**

Write an email to the chief executive, in 3 parts, in which you explain:

(a) (i) The main reasons for the sales revenue, material and labour variances from the flexed budget.

    (ii) How the sales revenue variance might have been avoided.

(b) How to set and manage a budget to drive improved performance.

(c) How the introduction of standard costing could assist effective budgetary control.

To: The Chief Executive   **From:** Budget Accountant
Subject: Review of Operating Statement   **Date:** xxxxxx

(a) **Reasons for variances**

(b) **Setting and managing the budget**

(c) **Standard costing**

AAT AQ2013 SAMPLE ASSESSMENT 1 BUDGETING

ANSWERS

Task 1 (16 marks)

(a)

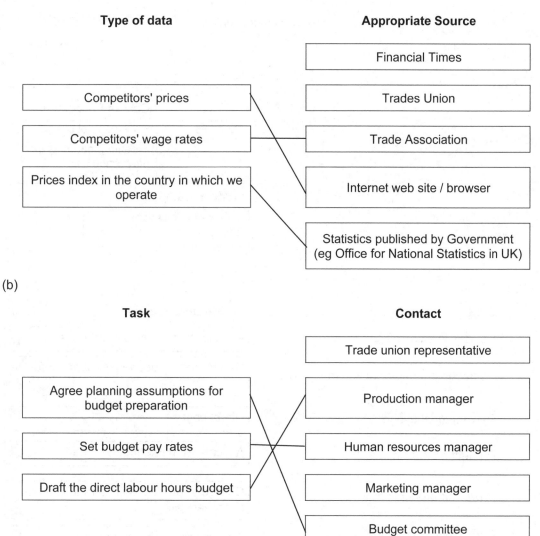

(b)

(c)

Capital expenditure

Replacement vehicles
for sales staff

Factory extension

Marketing & distribution

Sales force salaries

Hire of delivery vehicles

Cash Flow

Payments to suppliers

Cost of Production

Raw material usage

Cleaning materials for
production line

Administration

Telecommunications
charges

(d)

Cost	Accounting treatment
Repairs to sales office furniture	Allocate to marketing overheads ▼
Replacement of production machinery	Capitalise and depreciate over useful life ▼
Raw material usage	Direct cost ▼
Product advertising	Allocate to marketing overheads ▼
Power for production	Charge to production in a machine hour overhead rate ▼
Purchasing department	Activity based charge to products ▼
Production labour – idle time	Charge to production in a labour hour overhead rate ▼
Factory extension	Capitalise and depreciate over useful life ▼

(e)

Description	Term
A cost that fluctuates in direct proportion to changes in activity	Variable cost ▼
Detailed budgets prepared by functional managers are collated to form a master budget	Bottom up budgeting ▼
Collecting data about a proportion of the items in the population to indicate the characteristics of the whole population	Sampling ▼
A physical or financial measure to monitor efficiency, cost, quality, etc.	Performance indicator ▼

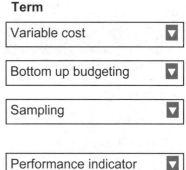

Drop-down list:

Variable cost / Fixed cost / Semi-variable cost / Stepped cost

Bottom up budgeting / Top down budgeting / Rolling budgets / Zero base budgeting / Incremental budgeting / Budget flexing / Budget revision

Sampling / Census / Stratified sampling / Trend / Market research / Market analysis / Product life cycle

Performance indicator / Variance / Performance review / Variance analysis / Material cost variance / Labour cost variance

··

Task 2 (19 marks)

(a)

Production (units)	Week 1	Week 2	Week 3	Week 4	Week 5
Sales volume	400	450	500	600	550
Opening inventory	75	57	63	75	
Closing inventory	57	63	75	69	
Saleable production	382	456	512	594	
Rejected production	68	81	91	105	
Total manufactured units	450	537	603	699	

(b) **How many litres are required for production?** 12,174 litres

How many litres must be purchased? 11,974 litres

(c) 834 hours

(d) **How many units must be subcontracted?** 410 units

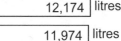

Task 3 (18 marks)

(a)

Materials	Kg	£
Opening inventory	50,000	60,000
Purchases	460,000	598,000
Sub-total	510,000	658,000
Used in production	441,750	569,275
Closing inventory	68,250	88,725

Labour	Hours	£
Basic time @ £16 per hour	24,000	384,000
Overtime	5,450	130,800
Total	29,450	514,800

Overhead	Hours	£
Variable @ £3.60 per hour	29,450	106,020
Fixed		105,705
Total		211,725

BPP
LEARNING MEDIA

(b)

Operating budget	Units	£ per unit	£
Sales revenue	600,000	2.35	1,410,000
Cost of goods sold:			£
Opening inventory of finished goods			150,000
Cost of production		£	
Materials		569,275	
Labour		514,800	
Overhead		211,725	1,295,800
Closing inventory of finished goods			179,080
Cost of goods sold			1,266,720
Gross profit			143,280
Overheads			
Administration		61,200	
Marketing		49,800	111,000

Use a negative figure to indicate a gross loss, for example –500 or (500).

Operating profit	32,280

Task 4 (17 marks)

(a)

Age range >>>	Up to 29	30 to 39	40 to 49	Over 49	Total
Number of customers	15,000	24,000	42,000	18,500	
Sample	181	289	507	223	1200

(b)

Budgeted units	Year	April
Units sold	216,000	18,200
Units produced	210,000	18,000

Budget in £	Year	April
Sales revenue	1,166,400	98,280
Material used	472,500	40,500
Direct labour	300,000	26,000
Variable production overhead	77,000	6,600
Fixed production overhead	13,200	1,100

(c)

Operating Budget	£	£
Sales revenue		103,000
Expenditure		
Materials	34,200	
Labour	38,500	
Other costs	16,400	89,100
Operating Profit		13,900

Cash Flow Forecast	£	£
Sales revenue		
Expenditure		
Materials	37,700	
Labour	38,500	
Other costs	11,600	87,800
Cash flow		12,700

Show a net cash outflow as a negative, for example –500.

Task 5 (20 marks)

(a) **Budget submission**

I attached the proposed raw materials budget for next year for your consideration and Approval. This year's results are shown for comparison.

This draft is based on the agreed production budget of 67,840 units which is 6% more than this year. However, the quantity of raw material purchases should increase by only 2.4%.

The material required in each unit of production will be unchanged at 0.4 kg. However, the production manager expects to reduce material from a more reliable supplier.

The purchasing manager supports this strategy but expects material price to rise by 5%.

Overall the material purchases budget shows an increase of 7.6%, compared with this year.

(b) **Performance indicators**

A number of assumptions have been made in this budget and we need to monitor their achievement.

Raw material costs are available and we should expect them to increase or decrease with production levels. I recommend that we review the following four indicators on a weekly basis.

- Material usage per unit of production
- Percentage of material wastage
- Price per kilo
- Number of days of material inventory

(c) **Forecasts**

Although the production manager should take ownership of this budget there are aspects of it which are not wholly within his control.

Purchase prices will be negotiated by the purchasing manager. The two managers need to work together to balance quality with price.

Wastage is an important factor and is at least partly dependent upon quality. The wastage level has been estimated for budget purposes and must be monitored carefully.

A reduction in inventory is planned. This will only be possible if the supplier proves to be more reliable, as anticipated.

Finally, the production manager cannot control production demand, although allowance for this can be made with budget flexing.

Task 6 (18 marks)

(a)

Operating Budget	First draft	Alternative Scenario
Sales price £ per unit	6.00	6.30
Sales volume	84,000	75,600
	£	£
Sales revenue	504,000	476,280
Costs		
Material	201,600	181,440
Labour	226,800	204,120
Energy	17,680	18,020
Depreciation	8,100	7,200
Total	454,180	410,780
Gross profit	49,820	65,500
Increase / (decrease) in gross profit		15,680

(b)

Activity data	Items produced	Hours	Cost
Budget	18,000	288,000	1,728,000
Actual results	17,000	280,500	1,626,900

Direct Labour Cost Statement	£
Standard direct labour cost of production	163,200
Variances (adverse shown as negative)	
Labour rate	56,100
Labour efficiency	–51,000
Labour cost	5,100

Task 7 (16 marks)

Monthly Operating Report

Original budget		Flexed budget	Actual	Variance Fav/(Adv)
178,000	Sales volume (units)		192,000	
£		£	£	£
1,281,600	Sales revenue	1,382,400	1,377,000	−5,400
	Costs			
462,800	Materials	499,200	500,100	−900
480,600	Labour	518,400	516,500	1,900
67,640	Distribution	72,960	74,200	−1,240
60,860	Energy	64,640	65,080	−440
24,000	Equipment hire	28,000	28,600	−600
8,800	Depreciation	8,800	8,700	100
78,000	Marketing	78,000	78,900	−900
25,600	Administration	25,600	24,820	780
1,208,300	Total	1,295,600	1,296,900	−1,300
73,300	Operating profit/(Loss)	86,800	80,100	−6,700

Task 8 (15 marks)

(a) Reasons for variances

I have reviewed the results for the period. There was an operating profit of £198,000 compared with the flexed budget profit of £196,000. The original budget anticipated a profit of £227,000 based on sales of 165,000 units.

Compared with the original budget, the result is disappointing and this is attributed to a loss of sales volume due to price competition. The volume was 11% below the original budget despite our own 10% price reduction during the year. The flexed budget calculations indicate that lost sales should have generated a profit of £31,000 (£227,000 less £196,000). The flexed budget is based on the original but with appropriate volume adjustments.

The unforeseen competition has taken sales volume from us and forced us to make 10% price reductions. The full year impact of the price reduction is significant and we are not confident that volume will recover fully. This situation might have been avoided with better market intelligence and a proactive marketing campaign.

Compared with the flexed budget there was an adverse sales variance of £29,000 (3.8%), caused by the 10% price reduction part way through the year.

However, there was a £9,000 favourable variance on material costs (4%) where both material price and usage were lower than budgeted. Similarly, the labour cost variance was £15,000 favourable (12%). With production volumes less than budgeted there was less need to work overtime at premium rate.

(b) Setting and managing the budget

To be challenging, budgets should be stretching, always striving for improvement, whilst being achievable. We can see from the operating statement that the adverse sales variance was counterbalanced by unrelated and fortuitous favourable cost variances in materials and labour. It can be argued that the budget was poorly focused, failing to address the threat of competition and not challenging managers to improve efficiency.

I recommend that we introduce closer scrutiny at the budget setting stage to ensure that budgetary slack is not permitted and that efficiency improvements are planned and introduced. A stretching budget is likely to motivate managers to improve performance. Variances need to be fully analysed and explained on a regular basis and corrective action taken promptly.

(c) Standard costing

Standard costing is an effective mechanism for bringing rigour to budgetary control. It makes sense to set standards for production resources at the level of a single unit of production. The standards can be multiplied by planned production levels to create cost budgets.

The system facilitates the calculation of detailed cost variances which helps managers to understand and manage the resources effectively. Looking at the operating statement, for example, we could analyse the material variance into the price and efficiency aspects and also see whether the labour variance was wholly due to saved overtime premium.

BPP
LEARNING MEDIA

AAT AQ2013 SAMPLE ASSESSMENT 2
BUDGETING

Time allowed: 2 hours

Task 1 (16 marks)

(a) Match each type of data with its appropriate source.

Click on a box in the left column then on one in the right column to indicate each answer. To remove a line, click on it.

Appropriate Source

Type of data

	Financial Times
Contact details for our customers	Customer relationship management system (CRM)
Competitor's productivity	Trade Association
Wages index for the country in which we operate	Internet website/browser
	Statistics published by Government (eg Office for National Statistics in UK)

(b) As budget accountant, match each task with the person or group that you will need to contact. Click on a box in the left column then on one in the right column to indicate each answer. To remove a line, click on it.

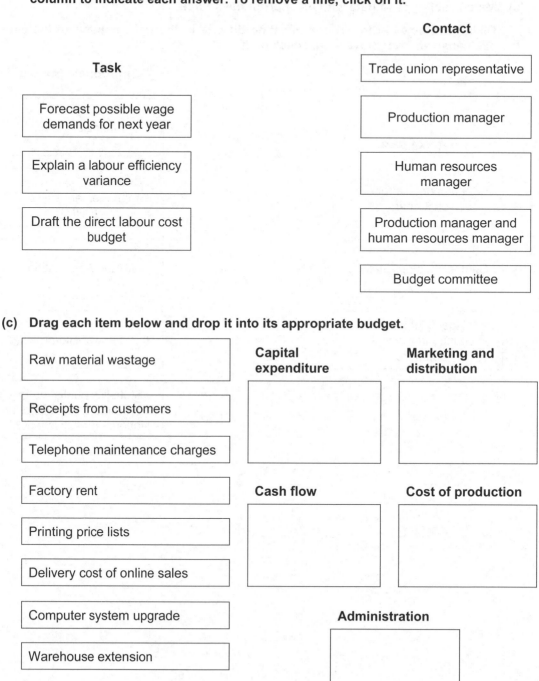

Contact

Task

Trade union representative

Forecast possible wage demands for next year

Production manager

Explain a labour efficiency variance

Human resources manager

Draft the direct labour cost budget

Production manager and human resources manager

Budget committee

(c) Drag each item below and drop it into its appropriate budget.

Raw material wastage

Capital expenditure

Marketing and distribution

Receipts from customers

Telephone maintenance charges

Factory rent

Cash flow

Cost of production

Printing price lists

Delivery cost of online sales

Computer system upgrade

Administration

Warehouse extension

(d) **Select the appropriate accounting treatment for each of the following costs.**

Cost	Accounting treatment
Customer survey (proposed new product)	▼
Upgrading production machinery	▼
Raw material wastage	▼
Import duty on raw materials	▼
Hire of production machinery	▼
Stores department	▼
Production labour - pension contribution	▼
Preparing plans for factory extension	▼

Drop-down list:

Allocate to marketing overheads
Charge to production in a machine hour overhead rate
Charge to production in a labour hour overhead rate
Direct cost
Activity based charge to products
Capitalise and depreciate over useful life

(e) **Select the appropriate term to match each of these descriptions.**

Description	Term
A cost that is fixed per unit of output	▼
Senior management prepare a master budget and delegate the responsibility for producing departmental budgets	▼
Collecting data about every item in the population	▼
A financial measure of the difference between budget and actual performance	▼

Drop-down lists:

(1) Variable cost / Fixed cost / Semi-variable cost / Stepped cost

(2) Bottom up budgeting / Top down budgeting / Rolling Budgets / Zero base budgeting / Incremental budgeting / Budget flexing / Budget revision

(3) Sampling / Census / Stratified sampling / Trend / Market research / Market analysis / Product life cycle

(4) Performance indicator / Variance / Performance review / Variance analysis / Material cost variance / Labour cost variance

Task 2 (19 marks)

(a) Complete the following production forecast for product F.

Do not show decimals. Round any decimal figures to the nearest whole number of units.

Closing inventory should be 15% of the following week's sales volume. 10% of all production fails quality control checks and is rejected.

Production (units)	Week 1	Week 2	Week 3	Week 4	Week 5
Sales volume	12,200	12,400	12,000	11,500	11,200
Opening inventory	1,750				
Closing inventory					
Saleable production					
Rejected production					
Total manufactured units					

(b) Calculate material purchases.

Do not show decimals. Round to the nearest whole number, if necessary.

- 4,000 items of product N are to be manufactured in April.
- Each requires 18 litres of raw material.
- 10% of raw material is wasted during manufacture.
- The opening inventory will be 7,600 litres.
- The closing inventory will be 6,800 litres.

(i) **How many litres will be used in production?**

| | litres

(ii) **How many litres must be purchased?**

| | litres

(c) Calculate overtime hours.

Do not show decimals. Round to the nearest whole number, if necessary.

- 3,280 items of product M are to be manufactured in May.
- Each one takes 45 minutes to produce.
- 12 staff will each work 180 basic hours.

How many overtime hours must be worked to complete the production?

| | hours

(d) Calculate the quantity to sub-contract.

Do not show decimals. Round to the nearest whole number, if necessary.

- 6,000 items of product S are to be manufactured in July.
- Each one takes 20 minutes to produce.
- 1,700 production hours are available.
- Any additional requirement must be sub-contracted.

How many units should be sub-contracted?

	units

....

Task 3 (18 marks)

You are required to complete the operating budget below.

Enter the missing figures in the working schedules and operating budget.

The production budget is to the right:

Production budget	Units
Opening inventory of finished goods	2,100
Production	17,400
Sub-total	19,500
Sales	18,000
Closing inventory of finished goods	1,500

(a) Complete these three working schedules.

Materials

Each unit produced requires 4kg of material. Closing inventory will be valued at the budgeted purchase price.

Materials	Kg	£
Opening inventory	3,400	4,930
Purchases	70,000	105,000
Sub-total	73,400	109,930
Used in production		
Closing inventory		

Labour

Each item takes 30 minutes to produce.
42 staff work 175 basic hours each in the period.
Overtime is paid at 50% above the basic hourly rate.

Labour	Hours	£
Basic time @ £16 per hour		
Overtime		
Total		

Overhead

Variable overhead is recovered on total labour hours.

Overhead	Hours	£
Variable @ £4.90 per hour		
Fixed		16,340
Total		

(b) Now complete the operating budget.

Enter income, costs and inventories as positive figures.

Operating budget	Units	£ per unit	£
Sales revenue		24.00	
Cost of goods sold:			£
Opening inventory of finished goods			29,000
Cost of production		£	
Materials			
Labour			
Overhead			

Closing finished goods inventory will be valued at the budgeted production cost per unit.

Operating budget	Units	£ per unit	£
Closing inventory of finished goods			
Cost of goods sold			
Gross profit/(loss)			
Overheads		£	
Administration		38,300	
Marketing		21,000	
Operating profit/(loss)			

••

Task 4 (17 marks)

(a) **Calculate a sales revenue forecast for year 5.**

Do not show decimals. Round to the nearest whole pound.

(i) Use the sales price index to calculate sales revenue for years 1 to 4 at year 1 prices.

(ii) Project the sales revenue at year 1 prices forward to year 5.

(iii) Calculate the year 5 sales revenue forecast.

	Year 1 Actual	Year 2 Actual	Year 3 Actual	Year 4 Actual	Year 5 Forecast
Sales revenue (£)	12,200	12,747	13,527	14,091	
Sales price index	110.0	114.0	120.0	124.0	130.0
Sales revenue at year 1 prices (£)					

(b) **Break sales revenue and cost budgets down into accounting periods.**

Prepare the budget for April using the information in the notes below.

Budgeted units	Year	April
Units sold	140,000	12,800
Units produced	150,000	12,500

Notes

- Each unit is made from 3 Kg of material costing £2.30 per Kg.

- It takes 12 minutes to make each item. 2,400 hours of basic time is available in the month. Any extra hours must be worked in overtime. The basic rate is £16 per hour. Overtime is paid at 25% above basic rate.

- Variable overhead relates to labour hours, including overtime. Fixed production overhead costs are incurred evenly through the year.

Budget in £	Year	April
Sales revenue	2,660,000	
Material used	1,035,000	
Direct labour	484,800	
Variable production overhead	217,500	
Fixed production overhead	94,800	

(c) Prepare the cash flow forecast from the operating budget and balance sheet assumptions.

Balance Sheet Assumptions

- Receivables will reduce by £500.
- Materials payables will increase by £2,000.
- Labour costs are paid in the period in which they are incurred.
- Other payables will reduce by £800.

Operating Budget	£	£
Sales revenue		88,000
Expenditure		
Materials	34,800	
Labour	25,700	
Other costs	14,900	75,400
Operating profit		12,600

Enter receipts and payments as positive figures.

Cash Flow Forecast	£	£
Sales receipts		
Payments		
Materials		
Labour		
Other costs		
Cashflow		

Enter a cash outflow as a negative figure eg –500

....

Task 5 (20 marks)

Budget submission

You have prepared a draft sales budget for the coming year.

Background information

- The sales volume (units) has been forecast by the sales manager.

- The business sells two products in its breakfast cereal range – the Fruityoats cereal with honey clusters and the Oatbran Surprise cereal with added fruit and fibre and less salt.

- Fruityoats has sold well for many years but sales are now falling due to changing consumer tastes and growing competition.

- Oatbran Surprise was introduced two years ago as a healthier option and is steadily growing in popularity.

- The sales manager says that reducing the price of Fruityoats will help to maintain sales. A price increase is proposed for Oatbran Surprise.

- A special marketing campaign is proposed to further boost the sales of Oatbran Surprise with an emphasis on its nutritional qualities.

Write an email to the budget committee, in three sections:

1. Submitting the budget for approval and explaining the key assumptions
2. Describing the major risks attached to the marketing campaign
3. Recommending four performance indicators, other than revenue and cost variances, to monitor the success of the strategy.

Draft Sales Budget	This Year Actual	Next Year Budget
Sales volume	Units	Units
Fruityoats	850,000	750,000
Oatbran Surprise	300,000	450,000
Selling price	£	£
Fruityoats	2.50	2.30
Oatbran Surprise	2.90	3.10
Sales revenue	£	£
Fruityoats	2,125,000	1,725,000
Oatbran Surprise	870,000	1,395,000
Total	2,995,000	3,120,000

To: The Budget Committee   **From:** Budget Accountant

Subject: Draft Sales Budget   **Date:** xx xx xx

1. **Budget submission**

2.   **Risk analysis**

3.   **Performance indicators**

Budget Accountant

Task 6 (18 marks)

This task is about budget revision.

You have submitted a draft operating budget to the budget committee. The committee has asked you to budget for an alternative scenario and calculate the increase or decrease in expected profit.

Alternative scenario

Reduce the selling price by 4%.
Increase the sales volume by 7.5%.
Revise the energy price rise to 2.5%.

Assumptions in the first scenario

Material and labour costs are variable.
Depreciation is a stepped cost, increasing at every 8,000 units.
There is an allowance for an energy price rise of 5%.

(a) **Complete the alternative scenario column in the operating budget table and calculate the increase or decrease in profit.**

   Apart from the sales price per unit, do not enter decimals. Round to the nearest whole number, if necessary.

Operating Budget	First Draft	Alternative Scenario
Sales price per unit (£)	50.00	
Sales volume	30,000	
	£	£
Sales revenue	1,500,000	
Costs		
Material	588,000	
Labour	522,000	
Energy	113,400	
Depreciation	39,200	
Total	1,262,600	
Gross profit	237,400	
Increase/(decrease) in gross profit		

(b) Variance analysis

Prepare the raw material cost statement from the activity data provided.

Activity data	Items produced	Kg used	Cost
Budget	63,000	31,500	94,500
Actual results	65,000	33,500	99,000

Raw material cost statement	£
Standard raw material cost of production	
Variances	£ fav/(adv)
Material price	
Material usage	
Material cost	

Task 7 (16 marks)

You are required to complete the monthly operating report below. Flex the budget, calculate variances and show whether each variance is favourable or adverse. The original budget and actual results have been entered.

Notes

Material, labour and distribution costs are variable.

Energy cost is semi-variable. The fixed element is budgeted at £24,000 per month.

Equipment hire is a stepped cost, budgeted to increase at every 20,000 units of monthly production.

Depreciation, marketing and administration costs are fixed.

Monthly Operating Report

Original budget		Flexed budget	Actual	Variance Fav/(Adv)
386,000	Sales volume (units)		410,000	
£		£	£	£
2,393,200	Sales revenue		2,516,300	
	Costs			
733,400	Materials		799,000	
791,300	Labour		838,900	
173,700	Distribution		182,600	
224,720	Energy		238,000	
80,000	Equipment hire		74,000	
39,700	Depreciation		38,600	
81,500	Marketing		86,700	
28,400	Administration		26,100	
2,152,720	Total		2,283,900	
240,480	Operating profit/(Loss)		232,400	

Task 8 (20 marks)

Operational review

Review the operating statement shown on the right and the additional information below, and prepare a report by email.

Additional information

- The budget has been flexed to the actual number of units produced and sold. The original budget was based on an expected sales volume of 750,000 units which was expected to generate a profit of £72,000.

- The original budget included £63,000 for depreciation of production machinery and £120,000 for the hire of additional machines to meet the budgeted workload. The plant engineer is responsible for both of these budgets. After the original budget was approved, he decided to purchase the additional production equipment rather than hire it. The depreciation cost was roughly the same as had been budgeted for equipment and so the standard cost of the product did not change.

- Early in the financial year the marketing manager increased the selling price of the product. He realised that this would reduce sales volume but estimated that profit would increase.

- The chief executive cannot understand how these important strategic decisions were made without his knowledge. He also wants to know why the standard cost of the product did not increase if depreciation was more expensive than equipment hire.

Write an email to the chief executive, in three sections, in which you explain:

1. (i) **The main reasons for the sales revenue, equipment hire and depreciation variances from the flexed budget.**

    (ii) **How the equipment hire and depreciation variances might have been avoided.**

2. **How failings in the budgetary control system resulted in lower profits.**

3. **Why the standard cost of the product did not increase when equipment was purchased rather than hired.**

Operating Statement	Flexed Budget	Actual	Variance Fav/(Adv)
Sales volume	608,000 units		
	£'000	£'000	£'000
Sales revenue	486	517	31
Variable costs			
Material	122	128	(6)
Labour	67	76	(9)
Distribution	24	21	3
Power	43	49	(6)
Equipment hire	97	0	97
Total	353	274	79
Contribution	133	243	110
Fixed costs			
Power	4	3	1
Depreciation	63	185	(122)
Marketing	11	15	(4)
Administration	14	15	(1)
Total	92	218	(126)
Operating profit	41	25	(16)

To: The Chief Executive   **From:**   Budget Accountant

Subject: Review of Operating Statement   **Date:**   xx xx xx

1. Reasons for variances

2. Budgetary control system failure

3. Standard cost

Budget Accountant

BPP
LEARNING MEDIA

AAT AQ2013 SAMPLE ASSESSMENT 2
BUDGETING

ANSWERS

Task 1 (16 marks)

(a) **Match each type of data with its appropriate source.**

Click on a box in the left column then on one in the right column to indicate each answer. To remove a line, click on it.

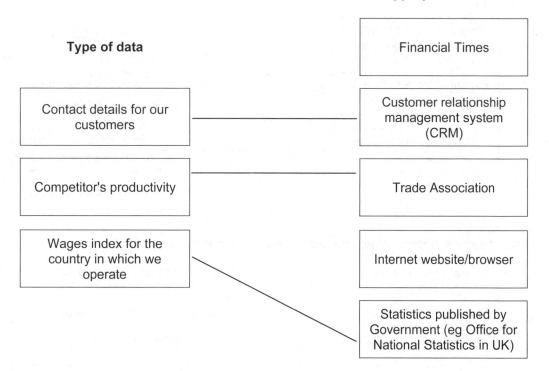

(b) As budget accountant, match each task with the person or group that you will need to contact. Click on a box in the left column then on one in the right column to indicate each answer. To remove a line, click on it.

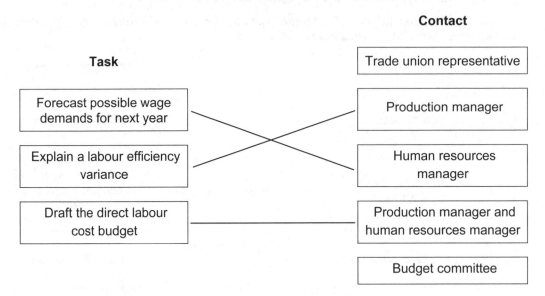

Contact

Task

Task	Contact
	Trade union representative
Forecast possible wage demands for next year	Production manager
Explain a labour efficiency variance	Human resources manager
Draft the direct labour cost budget	Production manager and human resources manager
	Budget committee

(c) Drag each item below and drop it into its appropriate budget.

Capital expenditure

Warehouse extension

Computer system upgrade

Marketing and distribution

Delivery cost of online sales

Printing price lists

Cash flow

Receipts from customers

Cost of production

Raw material wastage

Factory rent

Administration

Telephone maintenance charges

(d) Select the appropriate accounting treatment for each of the following costs.

Cost	Accounting treatment
Customer survey (proposed new product)	Allocate to marketing overheads ▼
Upgrading production machinery	Capitalise and depreciate over useful life ▼
Raw material wastage	Direct cost ▼
Import duty on raw materials	Direct cost ▼
Hire of production machinery	Charge to production in a machine hour overhead rate ▼
Stores department	Activity based charge to products ▼
Production labour – pension contribution	Charge to production in a labour hour overhead rate ▼
Preparing plans for factory extension	Capitalise and depreciate over useful life ▼

(e) Select the appropriate term to match each of these descriptions.

Description	Term
A cost that is fixed per unit of output	Variable cost ▼
Senior management prepare a master budget and delegate the responsibility for producing departmental budgets	Top down budgeting ▼
Collecting data about every item in the population	Census ▼
A financial measure of the difference between budget and actual performance	Variance ▼

Task 2 (19 marks)

(a) Complete the following production forecast for product F.

Do not show decimals. Round any decimal figures to the nearest whole number of units.

Closing inventory should be 15% of the following week's sales volume. 10% of all production fails quality control checks and is rejected.

Production (units)	Week 1	Week 2	Week 3	Week 4	Week 5
Sales volume	12,200	12,400	12,000	11,500	11,200
Opening inventory	1,750	1,860	1,800	1,725	
Closing inventory	1,860	1,800	1,725	1,680	
Saleable production	12,310	12,340	11,925	11,455	
Rejected production	1,368	1,371	1,325	1,273	
Total manufactured units*	13,678	13,711	13,250	12,728	

* Total manufactured units = Saleable production/90%

(b) Calculate material purchases.

Do not show decimals. Round to the nearest whole number, if necessary.

- 4,000 items of product N are to be manufactured in April.
- Each requires 18 litres of raw material.
- 10% of raw material is wasted during manufacture.
- The opening inventory will be 7,600 litres.
- The closing inventory will be 6,800 litres.

(i) **How many litres will be used in production?**

(4,000 × 18 litres)/90% = | 80,000 | litres

(ii) **How many litres must be purchased?**

Used in production	=	80,000
less		
Opening inventory	=	(7,600)
add		
Closing inventory	=	6,800
	=	79,200 litres

(c) Calculate overtime hours.

Do not show decimals. Round to the nearest whole number, if necessary.

- 3,280 items of product M are to be manufactured in May.
- Each one takes 45 minutes to produce.
- 12 staff will each work 180 basic hours.

How many overtime hours must be worked to complete the production?

| 300 | hours |

(d) Calculate the quantity to sub-contract.

Do not show decimals. Round to the nearest whole number, if necessary.

- 6,000 items of product S are to be manufactured in July.
- Each one takes 20 minutes to produce.
- 1,700 production hours are available.
- Any additional requirement must be sub-contracted.

How many units should be sub-contracted?

| 900 | units |

Task 3 (18 marks)

(a) **Complete these three working schedules.**

Materials

Each unit produced requires 4kg of material. Closing inventory will be valued at the budgeted purchase price.

Materials	Kg	£
Opening inventory	3,400	4,930
Purchases	70,000	105,000
Sub-total	73,400	109,930
Used in production	69,600	104,230
Closing inventory	3,800	5,700

Labour

Each item takes 30 minutes to produce.
42 staff work 175 basic hours each in the period.
Overtime is paid at 50% above the basic hourly rate.

Labour	Hours	£
Basic time @ £16 per hour	7,350	117,600
Overtime	1,350	32,400
Total	8,700	150,000

Overhead

Variable overhead is recovered on total labour hours.

Overhead	Hours	£
Variable @ £4.90 per hour	8,700	42,630
Fixed		16,340
Total		58,970

(b) Now complete the operating budget.

Enter income, costs and inventories as positive figures.

Closing finished goods inventory will be valued at the budgeted production cost per unit

Operating budget	Units	£ per unit	£
Sales revenue	18,000	24.00	432,000
Cost of goods sold:			£
Opening inventory of finished goods			29,000
Cost of production		£	
Materials		104,230	
Labour		150,000	
Overhead		58,970	313,200
Closing inventory of finished goods			27,000
Cost of goods sold			315,200
Gross profit/(loss)			116,800
Overheads		£	
Administration		38,300	
Marketing		21,000	59,300
Operating profit/(loss)			57,500

....

Task 4 (17 marks)

(a) Calculate a sales revenue forecast for year 5.

Do not show decimals. Round to the nearest whole pound.

(i)   Use the sales price index to calculate sales revenue for years 1 to 4 at year 1 prices.

(ii) Project the sales revenue at year 1 prices forward to year 5.

(iii) Calculate the year 5 sales revenue forecast.

	Year 1 Actual	Year 2 Actual	Year 3 Actual	Year 4 Actual	Year 5 Forecast
Sales revenue (£)	12,200	12,747	13,527	14,091	14,891
Sales price index	110.0	114.0	120.0	124.0	130.0
Sales revenue at year 1 prices (£)	12,200	12,300	12,400	12,500	

*Sales revenue at year 1 prices (£)

= Sales revenue year X (£) × Sales price index year (X–1)/Sales price index year X

(b) **Break sales revenue and cost budgets down into accounting periods.**

Prepare the budget for April using the information in the notes below.

Budgeted units	Year	April
Units sold	140,000	12,800
Units produced	150,000	12,500

Notes

- Each unit is made from 3 Kg of material costing £2.30 per Kg.

- It takes 12 minutes to make each item. 2,400 hours of basic time is available in the month. Any extra hours must be worked in overtime. The basic rate is £16 per hour. Overtime is paid at 25% above basic rate.

- Variable overhead relates to labour hours, including overtime. Fixed production overhead costs are incurred evenly through the year.

Budget in £	Year	April
Sales revenue	2,660,000	243,200
Material used	1,035,000	86,250
Direct labour	484,800	40,400
Variable production overhead	217,500	18,125
Fixed production overhead	94,800	7,900

(c) Prepare the cash flow forecast from the operating budget and balance sheet assumptions.

Balance Sheet Assumptions

- Receivables will reduce by £500.
- Materials payables will increase by £2,000.
- Labour costs are paid in the period in which they are incurred.
- Other payables will reduce by £800.

Operating Budget	£	£
Sales revenue		88,000
Expenditure		
Materials	34,800	
Labour	25,700	
Other costs	14,900	75,400
Operating profit		12,600

Enter receipts and payments as positive figures.

Cash Flow Forecast	£	£
Sales receipts		88,500
Payments		
Materials	32,800	
Labour	25,700	
Other costs	15,700	74,200
Cashflow		14,300

Enter a cash outflow as a negative figure eg –500

Task 5 (20 marks)

To: The Budget Committee   **Date:** xx xx xx
From: Budget Accountant   **Subject:** Draft Sales Budget

1. Budget submission

I attach the draft sales budget for your consideration and approval.

It is based on the sales manager's sales forecast and pricing proposal. This year's results are shown for comparison.

The Fruityoats cereal has sold well over the years but is now in the decline stage of its life-cycle and its volume is forecast to drop by 12%. To extend the product's life, in the face of competition, the sales manager proposes to reduce the price by £0.20 (8%).

The Oatbran Surprise cereal is steadily growing in popularity and is well into its growth stage. It commands a price premium which we propose to increase by £0.20 (7%). Despite this price increase it is forecast that sales will grow to 450,000 units (50%). However, we still need to maximise market awareness and a marketing campaign is planned to achieve this growth.

The revenue forecast is £1,725,000 for the Fruityoats cereal (down 19%), £3,120,000 for the Oatbran Surprise cereal (up 60%) and £3,120,000 in total (up 4.2%).

2. Risk analysis

The sales manager's strategy is to reduce the selling price of the Fruityoats cereal to help maintain sales. The combination of reduced unit contribution and declining volume will bring forward the date when the product is no longer viable.

With the two price changes, the price differential between the two products will increase and may adversely affect the sales of Oatbran Surprise. It is seen as a successor at a premium price and we should be encouraging customers to trade up.

Also, by increasing the price of the Oatbran Surprise this may deter customers buying the product and thus not hit the target sales figures resulting in less profit. We also need to bear in mind that the extra anticipated sales are intended to cover the special marketing campaign.

3. Performance indicators

We need to monitor both products for volume, price, market share and profitability. I recommend the following indicators are used:

- Weekly sales volume as a percentage increase or decrease on last year
- Average unit selling price versus budget
- Market share %
- Contribution per unit (variable costs to include promotion)

Budget Accountant

BPP
LEARNING MEDIA

Task 6 (18 marks)

This task is about budget revision.

You have submitted a draft operating budget to the budget committee. The committee has asked you to budget for an alternative scenario and calculate the increase or decrease in expected profit.

Alternative scenario

Reduce the selling price by 4%.
Increase the sales volume by 7.5%.
Revise the energy price rise to 2.5%.

Assumptions in the first scenario

Material and labour costs are variable.
Depreciation is a stepped cost, increasing at every 8,000 units.
There is an allowance for an energy price rise of 5%.

(a) **Complete the alternative scenario column in the operating budget table and calculate the increase or decrease in profit.**

Apart from the sales price per unit, do not enter decimals. Round to the nearest whole number, if necessary.

Operating Budget	First Draft	Alternative Scenario
Sales price per unit (£)	50.00	48.00
Sales volume	30,000	32,250
	£	£
Sales revenue	1,500,000	1,548,000
Costs		
Material	588,000	632,100
Labour	522,000	561,150
Energy	113,400	110,700
Depreciation	39,200	49,000
Total	1,262,600	1,352,950
Gross profit	237,400	195,050
Increase/(decrease) in gross profit		–42,350

(b) Variance analysis

Prepare the raw material cost statement from the activity data provided.

Activity data	Items produced	Kg used	Cost
Budget	63,000	31,500	94,500
Actual results	65,000	33,500	99,000

Raw material cost statement	£
Standard raw material cost of production	97,500
Variances	£ fav/(adv)
Material price	1,500
Material usage	–3,000
Material cost	–1,500

Task 7 (16 marks)

Monthly Operating Report

Original budget		Flexed budget	Actual	Variance Fav/(Adv)
386,000	Sales volume (units)	410,000		
£		£	£	£
2,393,200	Sales revenue	2,542,000	2,516,300	(25,700)
	Costs			
733,400	Materials	779,000	799,000	(20,000)
791,300	Labour	840,500	838,900	1,600
173,700	Distribution	184,500	182,600	1,900
224,720	Energy	237,200	238,000	(800)
80,000	Equipment hire	84,000	74,000	10,000
39,700	Depreciation	39,700	38,600	1,100
81,500	Marketing	81,500	86,700	(5,200)
28,400	Administration	28,400	26,100	2,300
2,152,720	Total	2,274,800	2,283,900	(9,100)
240,480	Operating profit/(Loss)	267,200	232,400	(34,800)

Task 8 (20 marks)

To:	The Chief Executive	Date:	xx xx xx
From:	Budget Accountant	Subject:	Review of Operating Statement

1. Reasons for variances

I have reviewed the results for the period. There was an operating profit of £25,000 compared with the flexed budget profit of £41,000. The original budget anticipated a profit of £72,000 based on sales of 750,000 units.

The favourable sales revenue variance over the flexed budget of £31 k (6.4%) was due to an unbudgeted price increase. A consequent reduction in sales volume was expected. It is worth noting that if costs had been kept to budget at this volume (the flexed budget shows £445,000 of variable and fixed costs) the profit would have been £72,000, exactly as originally budgeted.

However, expenditure exceeded the flexed budget. The plant engineer decided to purchase production equipment rather than hire. This gave a 100% saving in hire charges. The adverse variance on depreciation was £122k. At the originally budgeted production level the net variance would have been negligible. With a reduced volume it would have been possible to reduce the amount of equipment hired but the depreciation charge is fixed.

The variances on equipment hire and depreciation could have been avoided if the plant engineer had been aware of the expected volume reduction. Possibly he would have purchased less equipment. Possibly he would have decided against any purchase and continued hiring.

2. Budgetary control system failure

One of the uses of budgetary control is to create a mechanism for authorising management decisions and we seem to have overlooked this. Significant departures from the approved budget, such as the price reduction and the purchase of production equipment, need to be carefully considered, communicated and authorised.

Neither the marketing manager nor the plant engineer informed their colleagues about their plans. You, as chief executive did not authorise them. Whilst both decisions seemed reasonable in isolation the combined effect (reducing volume at the same time as replacing variable cost with fixed) hit profits.

This outcome would have been apparent if the budget had been revised to incorporate the new strategies. Furthermore it is disconcerting that the deterioration was not identified through regular management meetings.

3. Standard cost

Standard costing is an excellent system for controlling variable costs but not so useful for fixed overheads such as depreciation.

It is not surprising that the standard cost did not change when the plant engineer decided to purchase equipment if he was not aware that volume would reduce. At the original budget volume, £120,000 of equipment hire would have been replaced a similar amount of depreciation. The unit cost would be the same.

In time the reduced volume would generate an under recovery of overheads but, as the budget had not been revised, it would not be easy to see what was going wrong.

Budget Accountant

....

BPP PRACTICE ASSESSMENT 1
BUDGETING

Time allowed: 2.5 hours

Task 1a

Match each type of data with its appropriate source.

(CBT instructions: Click on a box in the left column, then on one in the right column. To remove a line, click on it.)

Type of data	Appropriate Source
Corporation Tax rates	Trade Union
Competitors' financial performance	HM Revenue & Customs
Inflation rates	Financial Times
	Internet web site/browser
	Statistics published by Government (eg Office for National Statistics in UK)

Task 1b

As budget accountant, match each task with the person or group that you will need to contact.

(CBT instructions: Click on a box in the left column, then on one in the right column. To remove a line, click on it.)

Task	Contact
Obtain details of salaries for proposed new staff	Budget committee
Agree variance reports required for budget	Marketing manager
Draft the direct materials budget	Human resources manager
	Trade union representative
	Production manager

Task 1c

Drag each item below and drop it into its appropriate budget.

- Capital expenditure
- Marketing & distribution
- Cash Flow
- Cost of Production
- Administration

The drag and drop choices are:

- Client entertaining at rugby match
- Repair of damaged lighting system at head office
- Receipts from customers
- Purchase of new production plant
- Raw materials
- Bonus for production staff
- Hire of office printers
- Depreciation of factory equipment

Classification	Expenditure
Capital expenditure	
Marketing & distribution	
Cash Flow	
Cost of Production	
Administration	

Task 1d

Select the appropriate accounting treatment for each of the following costs.

Cost	Accounting treatment
Repairs to head office furniture	▼
Water used directly in production	▼
Head office extension	▼
Raw material purchases	▼
Production labour – overtime pay	▼
Replacement of head office IT system	▼
Machine maintenance	▼
Cost of the head office canteen	▼

Picklist:

Allocate to administration overheads

Capitalise and depreciate over useful life

Direct cost

Charge to production in a machine hour overhead rate

Activity based charge to products

Task 1e

Select the appropriate term to match each of these descriptions.

Description	Term
A cost which does not change as activity levels alter.	▼
A budget that is continuously updated by adding a further accounting period each time the current accounting period is completed.	▼
Cost or income data collected over a number of periods, which may be used as a basis for forecasting.	▼
A budget that is set in advance of a period, whose purpose is to provide a single achievable target for the entire organisation to work to.	▼

Picklist:

Time series

Rolling budget

Fixed cost

Fixed budget

Task 2a

Complete the following production forecast for product J based on the information below. Do not show decimals. Round any decimal figures *up to the next whole number* of units.

Closing inventory should be 12.5% of the following week's sales volume.

17.5% of saleable production fails quality control checks and is rejected.

Production (units)	Week 1	Week 2	Week 3	Week 4	Week 5
Sales volume	500	550	600	650	700
Opening inventory	100				
Closing inventory					
Saleable production					
Rejected production					
Total manufactured units					

Task 2b

Calculate raw material requirements.

Do not show decimals. Round any decimal figures *up to the next whole number* of litres.

900 units of product N are to be manufactured next week.

Each requires 15 litres of raw material.

9% of raw material is wasted during manufacture.

The opening inventory will be 500 litres.

The closing inventory will be 600 litres.

How many litres are required for production? ☐ litres

How many litres must be purchased? ☐ litres

Task 2c

Calculate Labour hours.

Do not show decimals. Round any decimal figures *up to the next whole number* of hours.

60,000 items of product F are to be delivered in May.

Each one of them takes 3 minutes to produce.

10 staff will each work 200 basic hours.

How many overtime hours must be worked to complete the production?

| | hours
|---|

....

Task 2d

Calculate sub-contracting requirements.

Do not show decimals. Round any decimal figures *up to the next whole number* of units.

8,000 items of product R are to be manufactured next week.

Each one takes 3 minutes to produce.

320 production labour hours are available.

Any additional requirement must be sub-contracted.

How many units must be sub-contracted?

| | units
|---|

....

Task 3a

Operating budget

Enter the missing figures in the working schedules and operating budget using the data from the production budget and the notes below.

Production budget	Units
Opening inventory of finished goods	40,000
Production	320,000
Sub-total	360,000
Sales	310,000
Closing inventory of finished goods	50,000

Complete these three working schedules.

Materials

Each unit requires 0.75kg of material.

Closing inventory will be valued at the budgeted purchase price.

Materials	Kg	£
Opening inventory	40,000	50,000
Purchases	250,000	300,000
Subtotal	290,000	350,000
Used in production		
Closing inventory		

Labour

Each item takes 6 minutes to produce.

150 staff work 150 basic hours each in the period.

Overtime is paid at 50% above the basic hourly rate.

Labour	Hours	£
Basic time @ £15 per hour		
Overtime		
Total		

Overhead

Variable overhead is recovered on total labour hours.

Overhead	Hours	£
Variable @ £2.50 per hour		
Fixed		70,750
Total		

Task 3b

Now complete the operating budget.

Enter income, costs and inventories as positive figures.

Closing finished goods inventory will be valued at the budgeted production cost per unit.

Use a negative figure to indicate a gross loss, for example -500 or (500).

Use a negative figure to indicate an operating loss, for example -500 or (500).

Operating budget	Units	£ per unit	£
Sales revenue		£3.50	
Cost of goods sold:			£
Opening inventory of finished goods			120,000
Cost of production		£	
Materials			
Labour			
Overhead			
Closing inventory of finished goods			
Cost of goods sold			
Gross profit			
Overheads		£	
Administration		29,200	
Marketing		30,800	
Operating profit			

Task 4a

Stratified sampling

Calculate the number of customers to be interviewed from each age group to obtain a representative response from 1,600 interviews.

Do not show decimals. Round to the nearest whole number.

	Up to 29	30 to 39	40 to 49	Over 49	Total
Number of customers	13,000	21,000	41,000	17,000	
Sample					

Task 4b

Break a budget down into accounting periods

Calculate the sales revenue and cost budgets for April using the budgeted unit data and the information below.

Do not show decimals. Round to the nearest whole number.

- Each unit is made from 2kg of material costing £1.25 per kg.

- It takes 3 minutes to make each item.

- 650 hours of basic time is available in the month. Any extra hours must be worked in overtime.

- The basic rate is £12 per hour. Overtime is paid at 50% above basic rate.

- Variable overhead relates to labour hours, including overtime.

- Fixed production overhead costs are spread evenly throughout the year.

Budgeted units	Year	April
Units sold	200,000	18,000
Units produced	190,000	17,800

Budget in £	Year	April
Sales revenue	1,100,000	
Material used	475,000	
Direct labour	124,200	
Variable production overhead	60,000	
Fixed production overhead	14,400	

Task 4c

Cash flow forecast

Prepare the forecast from the operating budget and statement of financial position (balance sheet) assumptions.

Enter receipts and payments as positive figures.

Statement of financial position (balance sheet) assumptions:

- Receivables will increase by £1,000.
- Materials payables will reduce by £1,400.
- Labour costs are paid in the period in which they are incurred.
- Other payables will increase by £4,300.

Operating budget	£	£
Sales revenue		100,000
Expenditure:		
Materials	23,100	
Labour	32,300	
Other costs	12,600	68,000
Operating profit		32,000

Cash flow forecast (to be completed)	£	£
Sales receipts		
Payments:		
Materials		
Labour		
Other costs		
Cash flow		

Task 5

Budget submission

You have prepared a draft labour budget for the coming year.

Background information

- The production budget (units) has already been agreed.

- The managing director is pleased as he thinks greater output means the workers will be more efficient.

Draft direct labour budget	This year Actual	Next year Budget
Production (units)	428,000	467,800
Units per labour hour	0.67	0.62
Labour		
Required for production (hours)	642,000	748,500
Labour hours @ Standard rate	500,000	500,000
Labour cost @ Standard rate (£10/hour)	£5,000,000	£5,000,000
Labour hours @ Overtime rate	142,000	248,500
Labour cost @ Overtime rate (£15/hour)	£2,130,000	£3,727,500
Direct labour cost total (£)	**£7,130,000**	**£8,727,500**

Write an email to the budget committee, in 2 parts:

(a) **Requesting approval for the budget and explaining the assumptions upon which it is based.**

(b) **Suggesting and explaining performance measures or indicators that could be used to investigate the performance of workers.**

To: The Budget Committee   **From:** Budget Accountant
Subject: Draft Labour Budget   **Date:** xxxxxx

(a) **Budget submission**

(b) **Performance indicators**

Budget Accountant

Task 6a

Budget revision

You have submitted a draft operating budget to the budget committee. The committee has asked you to budget for an alternative scenario and calculate the increase or decrease in expected profit.

Complete the alternative scenario column in the operating budget table and calculate the increase or decrease in profit.

Assumptions in the first scenario

Material and labour costs are variable.

Depreciation is a stepped cost, increasing at every 8,000 units.

There is an allowance for an energy price rise of 3%.

Alternative scenario

Increase the selling price by 5%

Reduce the sales volume by 8%

Revise the energy price rise to 6%

Apart from sales price per unit, do not enter decimals.

Round to the nearest whole number, if necessary.

Operating budget	First draft	Alternative scenario
Sales price £ per unit	5.00	
Sales volume	110,000	
	£	£
Sales revenue	550,000	
Costs:		
Materials	216,000	
Labour	207,300	
Energy	16,995	
Depreciation	8,400	
Total	448,695	
Gross profit	101,305	
Increase/(decrease) in gross profit		

Task 6b

Variance analysis

Prepare the direct labour cost statement from the activity data provided

Enter favourable variances as positive figures – for example 500.

Enter adverse variances as negative figures – for example –500.

Activity data	Items produced	Labour hours	Cost (£)
Budget	36,000	576,000	3,456,000
Actual results	34,000	561,000	3,253,800

Direct labour cost statement	£
Standard direct labour cost of production	
Variances (adverse shown as negative)	
Labour rate	
Labour efficiency	
Labour cost	

Task 7

Monthly operating report

The budgeted and actual performance for a month is given below.

Flex the budget to the actual activity level, given the information below about costs, and show whether each variance is favourable or adverse.

Enter favourable variances as positive figures – for example 500.

Enter adverse variances as negative figures – for example –500.

Original Budget		Flexed budget	Actual	Variance Fav/(Adv)
36,000	Sales volume (units)		35,000	
£		£	£	£
1,440,000	Sales revenue		1,365,000	
	Costs			
432,000	Material		437,500	
216,000	Labour		203,000	
92,000	Light, heat, power		85,500	
100,000	Depreciation		70,000	
220,000	Administration		230,000	
180,000	Marketing		190,000	
1,240,000	Total		1,216,000	
200,000	Operating profit/(Loss)		149,000	

Material and labour costs are variable.

The costs for light, heat and power are semi-variable. The budgeted fixed element is £20,000.

The budget for marketing costs is stepped, increasing every 10,000 units.

Depreciation and administration costs are fixed.

....

Task 8

Operational review

Review the operating statement shown and the additional information below, and prepare a report by email.

Additional information

At the end of the previous year a new warehouse had been purchased which has meant a saving in warehouse rental.

Six new machines were installed at the start of the year which are more power-efficient than the old machines, but also more expensive, causing a larger depreciation charge.

There was an unexpected increase in the materials price during the year and when other suppliers were contacted it was found that they were all charging approximately the same higher price for the materials.

A higher than normal skilled grade of labour was used during the year due to staff shortages. The production process is a skilled process and the benefit has been that these employees, although more expensive, have produced the goods faster and with less wastage. This particular group of employees is also keen to work overtime and, as the business wishes to build up inventory levels, advantage of this has been taken.

The original budget was prepared by a management committee and approved by the Chief Executive. She is pleased that profit is higher than originally budgeted, but asks you how she can encourage the management team to perform even better in the future.

Operating Statement	Flexed Budget	Actual	Variance Fav(Adv)
Sales volume	21,300 units		
	£'000	£'000	£'000
Sales revenue	670	680	10
Variable costs			
Material	185	205	(20)
Labour	92	94	(2)
Distribution	30	30	–
Power	15	15	–
Equipment hire	78	79	(1)
Total	400	423	(23)
Contribution	270	257	(13)
Fixed costs			
Power	70	40	30
Depreciation	15	35	(20)
Rent	70	48	22
Marketing	25	25	–
Administration	20	20	–
Total	200	168	30
Operating profit	70	89	19

Write an email to the chief executive, in 3 parts, in which you explain:

(a) (i) What effect the combination of the factors given above might have had on the fixed costs, materials and labour variances from the flexed budget.

(ii) Any action that should be taken in light of these factors.

(b) The steps that should be taken when setting budgets, if they are to be successful in motivating staff.

(c) Why managers should be held responsible for controllable costs only.

To: The Chief Executive **From:** Budget Accountant
Subject: Review of Operating Statement **Date:** xxxxxx

(a) **Effect of factors on variances**

(b) **Steps if budgets are to motivate**

(c) **Controllable costs**

BPP PRACTICE ASSESSMENT 1 BUDGETING

ANSWERS

Task 1a

Type of data	Appropriate Source
Corporation Tax rates	Trade Union
Competitors' financial performance	HM Revenue & Customs
Inflation rates	Financial Times
	Internet web site/browser
	Statistics published by Government (eg Office for National Statistics in UK)

Task 1b

Task	Contact
Obtain details of salaries for proposed new staff	Budget committee
Agree variance reports required for budget	Marketing manager
Draft the direct materials budget	Human resources manager
	Trade union representative
	Production manager

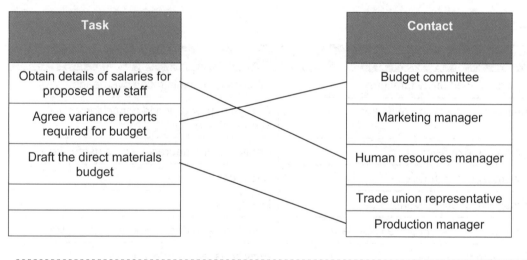

Task 1c

Expenditure	Classification
Capital expenditure	Purchase of new production plant
Marketing & distribution	Client entertaining at rugby match
Cash Flow	Receipts from customers
Cost of Production	Raw materials
	Bonus for production staff
	Depreciation of factory equipment
Administration	Repair of damaged lighting system at head office
	Hire of office printers

Task 1d

Cost	Accounting treatment
Repairs to head office furniture	Allocate to administration overheads
Water used directly in production	Charge to production in a machine hour overhead rate
Head office extension	Capitalise and depreciate over useful life
Raw material purchases	Direct cost
Production labour – overtime pay	Direct cost
Replacement of head office IT system	Capitalise and depreciate over useful life
Machine maintenance	Activity based charge to products
Cost of the head office canteen	Allocate to administration overheads

Task 1e

Description	Term
A cost which does not change as activity levels alter.	Fixed cost
A budget that is continuously updated by adding a further accounting period each time the current accounting period is completed.	Rolling budget
Cost or income data collected over a number of periods, which may be used as a basis for forecasting.	Time series
A budget that is set in advance of a period, whose purpose is to provide a single achievable target for the entire organisation to work to.	Fixed budget

Task 2a

Production (units)	Week 1	Week 2	Week 3	Week 4	Week 5
Sales volume	500	550	600	650	700
Opening inventory	100	69	75	82	
Closing inventory	69	75	82	88	
Saleable production	469	556	607	656	
Rejected production	83	98	107	115	
Total manufactured units	552	654	714	771	

You are given the opening inventory figure, so can calculate the closing and opening inventory figures for the rest of the five weeks. From this, with sales, you can calculate the saleable production figures (sales + closing inventory – opening inventory = saleable production). You can then calculate the figures for rejected production and for total manufactured units.

Task 2b

How many litres are required for production?   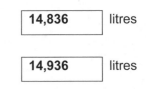   14,836 litres

How many litres must be purchased?   14,936 litres

Working	
Units manufactured	900
× 15 litres each	13,500
÷ 91% = total litres required	14,836
Opening inventory	(500)
Closing inventory	600
Total manufactured units	14,936

Task 2c

The correct answer is: **1,000**

Workings

60,000 items × 3 minutes each = 180,000 minutes of labour required

180,000 minutes ÷ 60 = 3,000 hours of labour required

200 × 10 = 2,000 basic hours available

3,000 – 2,000 = 1,000 hours overtime required

··

Task 2d

The correct answer is: **1,600**

8,000 items × 3 minutes = 24,000 minutes

24,000 minutes ÷ 60 = 400 hours needed

400 hours needed – 320 hours available = 80 hours to be sub-contracted

80 hours × 60 = 4,800 minutes to be sub-contracted

4,800 minutes ÷ 3 = 1,600 units to be sub-contracted

··

Task 3a

Materials	Kg	£
Opening inventory	40,000	50,000
Purchases	250,000	300,000
Subtotal	290,000	350,000
Used in production	240,000 *W1*	290,000
Closing inventory	50,000	60,000 *W2*

Workings

W1 Production materials = 320,000 × 0.75 = 240,000

W2 Closing inventory = 50,000 × 300,000/250,000

Labour	Hours	£
Basic time @ £15 per hour	22,500 *W3*	337,500
Overtime	9,500	213,750 *W5*
Total	32,000 *W4*	551,250

Workings

W3 Basic hours = 150 staff × 150 hours = 22,500

W4 Total labour required = 320,000 ÷ 10 = 32,000 hours

W5 Overtime = 9,500 × £15 × 1.5

Overhead	Hours	£
Variable @ £2.50 per hour	32,000	80,000
Fixed		70,750
Total		150,750

Task 3b

Operating budget	Units	£ per unit	£
Sales revenue	310,000	£3.50	1,085,000
Cost of goods sold:			£
Opening inventory of finished goods (40,000 units)			120,000
Cost of production		£	
Materials		290,000	
Labour		551,250	
Overhead		150,750	992,000
Closing inventory of finished goods			
Cost of goods sold			957,000
Gross profit			128,000
Overheads		£	
Administration		29,200	
Marketing		30,800	60,000
Operating profit			68,000

W1 Closing inventory of finished goods

Budgeted production cost per unit is £992,000 ÷ 320,000 units = £3.10/unit.

Hence closing inventory of finished goods is valued at 50,000 units × £3.10 = £155,000.

....

Task 4a

	Up to 29	30 to 39	40 to 49	Over 49	Total
Number of customers	13,000	21,000	41,000	17,000	92,000
Sample	226	365	713	296	1,600

Workings

Up to 29	13,000 / 92,000 × 1,600	226
30 to 39	21,000 / 92,000 × 1,600	365
40 to 49	41,000 / 92,000 × 1,600	713
Over 49	17,000 / 92,000 × 1,600	296

Task 4b

Budgeted units	Year	April
Units sold	200,000	18,000
Units produced	190,000	17,800

Budget in £	Year	April
Sales revenue	1,100,000	99,000 *W1*
Material used	475,000	44,500 *W2*
Direct labour	124,200	12,120 *W3*
Variable production overhead	60,000	5,621 *W4*
Fixed production overhead	14,400	1,200

Workings

W1

Price = £1,100,000 ÷ 200,000 = £5.50/unit

£5.50 × 18,000 units = £99,000

W2

17,800 units × 2kg × £1.25/kg = £44,500

W3

Labour hours required = 17,800 units × 3 minutes ÷ 60mins/hour = 890 hours

650 hours @ £12/hr = £7,800

240 hours @ £12/hr × 1.5 = £4,320

Total = £7,800 + £4,320 = £12,120

W4

Variable production overhead for April = £60,000 × 890 hours / total annual labour hours

Total annual labour hours = 190,000 × 3 ÷ 60 = 9,500 hours

Hence £60,000 × 890/9500 = £5,621

Task 4c

Operating budget	£	£
Sales revenue		100,000
Expenditure:		
Materials	23,100	
Labour	32,300	
Other costs	12,600	68,000
Operating profit		32,000

Cash flow forecast (to be completed)	£	£
Sales receipts		99,000
Payments:		
Materials	24,500	
Labour	32,300	
Other costs	8,300	65,100
Cash flow		33,900

Task 5

To:	The Budget Committee	From:	Budget Accountant
Subject:	Draft Labour Budget	Date:	xxxxxx

(a) **Budget submission**

I attach the proposed labour budget for next year for your consideration and approval. This year's results are shown for comparison.

This draft is based on the agreed production of 467,800 units, which is 9% more than this year. However, the total number of labour hours is expected to rise from 642,000 to 748,500, which is 17%.

The number of labour hours worked at the Standard rate will remain constant at 500,000 hours. The increase in the total labour hours needed will be met by a rise in overtime hours of 75%, from 142,000 hours to 248,500 hours. Overtime payments will increase by £1,597,500.

Overall the direct labour budget shows an increase of 22% compared with this year.

(b) **Performance indicators**

A possible productivity performance measure is units produced per hour compared with budget. This year's figures are 0.67 units/hour, while next year's budget is for 0.62 units/hour. This means that the workers are expected to work less efficiently than during this year.

You could also look at productivity in terms of units produced per employee.

The budgeted number of hours is greater than this year's actual hours, suggesting either an increased number of employees or existing workers working overtime. You can therefore also use the number of employees compared with budgeted performance and the number of basic hours, and overtime hours compared with budget.

Further analysis could then look at productivity of new versus existing employees (ie the number produced per employee for each of these two categories). The learning effect may improve the productivity of new employees with time.

Alternatively if overtime was worked, you could compare the number produced per basic labour hour, with the number produced per overtime hour (which may be less if workers are fatigued from long shifts).

Budget Accountant

Task 6a

Operating budget	First draft	Alternative scenario	Working
Sales price £ per unit	5.00	5.25	*5 × 1.05*
Sales volume	110,000	101,200	*110,000 × 0.92*
	£	£	
Sales revenue	550,000	531,300	*5.25 × 101,200*
Costs:			
Materials	216,000	198,720	*216,000 × 0.92*
Labour	207,300	190,716	*207,300 × 0.92*
Energy	16,995	17,490	*16,995/1.03 × 1.06*
Depreciation	8,400	7,800	*W1*
Total	448,695	414,726	
Gross profit	101,305	116,574	
Increase/(decrease) in gross profit		15,269	

Workings

W1

Depreciation is in steps of 8,000 by volume. Therefore the charge at volume of 110,000 puts this at the 14th step. Each step is therefore £8,400 ÷ 14 = £600.

A volume of 101,200 ÷ 8,000 = 12.65, ie the 13th step. £600 × 13 = £7,800.

• •

Task 6b

Direct labour cost statement	£
Standard direct labour cost of production	3,264,000 *W1*
Variances (adverse shown as negative)	
Labour rate	112,200 *W2*
Labour efficiency	−102,000 *W3*
Labour cost	10,200

Workings

W1

3,456,000 ÷ 36,000 = £96

£96 × 34,000 = £3,264,000

W2

Standard rate = 3,456,000 ÷ 576,000 = £6.00/hr

Actual rate = 3,253,800 ÷ 561,000 = £5.80/hr

Labour rate variance = (£6 − £5.80) × 561,000 = £112,200

Variance is favourable − actual rate is lower than budget.

W3

Standard efficiency = 576,000 ÷ 36,000 = 16hrs/unit

Actual efficiency = 561,000 ÷ 34,000 = 16.5hrs/unit

Labour efficiency variance = (16 − 16.5) × £6/hr × 34,000 = −£102,000

Variance is adverse − actual efficiency is worse than budget (more hours per unit).

Task 7

Original Budget		Flexed budget	Actual	Variance
36,000	Sales volume (units)	35,000	35,000	
£		£	£	£
1,440,000	Sales revenue (W1)	1,400,000	1,365,000	−35,000 A
	Costs			
432,000	Material (W2)	420,000	437,500	−17,500 A
216,000	Labour (W3)	210,000	203,000	7,000 F
92,000	Light, heat, power (W4)	90,000	85,500	4,500 F
100,000	Depreciation	100,000	70,000	30,000 F
220,000	Administration	220,000	230,000	−10,000 A
180,000	Marketing (W5)	180,000	190,000	−10,000 A
1,240,000	Total	1,220,000	1,216,000	−4,000 A
200,000	Operating profit/(Loss)	180,000	149,000	−31,000 A

Workings

1. Budgeted selling price per unit

   Revenue (turnover)/sales volume

   £1,440,000/36,000 = £40

   Flexed budget: 35,000 × £40 = £1,400,000

2. Budgeted material cost

   £432,000/36,000 = £12

   Flexed budget: 35,000 × £12 = £420,000

3. Budgeted labour cost

   £216,000/36,000 = £6

   Flexed budget: 35,000 × £6 = £210,000

4. Budgeted light, heat, power cost.

   Fixed element = £20,000

   Original budget, variable element = £92,000 − £20,000 = £72,000

   Variable element per unit = £72,000/36,000 = £2 per unit

   Flexed budget variable element 35,000 × £2 = £70,000

   Total flexed cost = £20,000 + £70,000 = £90,000

5. Budgeted marketing cost is stepped, but original and flexed budget in the same range so flexed budget = £180,000.

Task 8

To: The Chief Executive   **From:** Budget Accountant
Subject: Review of Operating Statement   **Date:** xxxxxx

(a) **Effect of factors on variances**

I have reviewed the results for the period. There was an operating profit of £89,000, compared with a flexed budget profit of £70,000. This represents a favourable variance of £19,000.

New warehouse – this will have the effect of reducing the rent expense but increasing the depreciation expense. The favourable rent expense variance of £22,000 appears to be a result of this.

New machines – the new machines use less power than the old ones, and therefore reduce the power expense. This appears to have resulted in a favourable power variance of £30,000. There will, however, be an increase in the depreciation charge as a result of the new machines.

Taken together, both the new warehouse and the new machines have contributed to the adverse depreciation variance of £20,000. Each of these changes has individually resulted in favourable variances (£22,000 and £30,000) that are greater than the combined adverse depreciation variance, so the changes both appear to have been beneficial.

Once the reduction in rent and power costs, and the increase in depreciation charge, are known then the standard fixed overhead should be adjusted.

Price increase – the price increase will be a cause of the adverse materials variance. The price increase appears to be a permanent one as all suppliers have increased their prices so the standard materials cost should be altered.

Skilled labour – the use of the higher skilled labour would be expected to have a favourable effect on the labour efficiency variance. The additional expense of the skilled labour and the overtime that has been worked will have had an adverse effect on the labour rate variance, which has cancelled out the effect of the increased labour efficiency to leave a small adverse labour variance. Unless the use of this grade of labour is likely to be a permanent policy then there should be no change to the standard labour rate or hours.

The use of the higher skilled labour would also have a favourable effect on the materials variance due to decreased wastage. However, the adverse effect of the increased price much exceeds this positive effect on materials, leading to the £20,000 adverse variance.

(b) **Steps if budgets are to motivate**

Managers should participate in setting the budgets.

The budgets should be agreed with all parties.

Targets should be challenging but attainable.

All known external (non-controllable) factors should be included in the forecasts.

Managers should be appraised only on costs within their budget which they can control.

Budgets should be reviewed during the period to which they relate, and revised for factors beyond the control of managers.

(c) **Controllable costs**

Operations managers can only be responsible in the short term for variances arising from their own decisions, rather than from factors outside their control such as inaccuracies in overall planning.

If costs, revenues and variances are reported as part of the responsibility of a manager but in fact he or she has no control, then this can have a de-motivational effect.

Looking at the operating statement, for example, if an operations manager were to be assessed on the basis of the adverse materials variance, then this would likely be de-motivational as the cause of that adverse variance lay outside of that manager's control.

BPP PRACTICE ASSESSMENT 2
BUDGETING

Time allowed: 2.5 hours

Task 1a

A factory has two production departments, assembly and finishing.

Match the factory overheads (on the left) with the most appropriate method of attributing these overheads between the two departments.

(CBT instructions: Click on a box in the left column, then on one in the right column. To remove a line, click on it.)

Overheads
Rent and rates
Canteen expenses
Inventory insurance

Method of allocation
Number of staff employed
Floor area
Units produced
Average inventory held

Task 1b

As budget accountant, match each task with the person or group that you will need to contact.

(CBT instructions: Click on a box in the left column, then on one in the right column. To remove a line, click on it.)

Task
Draft the direct labour budget
Draft the advertising budget
Obtain details of machinery to be purchased in the coming year
Obtain details of staff redundancies
Agree deadlines for production of budgets

Contact
Budget committee
Marketing manager
Human resources manager
Trade union representative
Production manager

Task 1c

Drag each item below and drop it into its appropriate budget.

- Legal fees regarding late payment by customers
- Advertising costs
- Cost of new computer system for office
- Depreciation costs of new computer system
- Cost of annual audit
- Wastage costs incurred on production line

The drag and drop choices are:
- Labour
- Material
- Sales and marketing
- Administration
- Capital

Classification	Expenditure
Labour	
Material	
Sales and marketing	
Administration	
Capital	

Task 1d

Select the appropriate accounting treatment for each of the following costs.

Cost	Accounting treatment
Purchase of latest version of IT software package	▼
Cost of new marketing materials	▼
Client entertaining at football match	▼
Company cars provided to sales team	▼
Legal costs of buying new factory	▼
Buildings insurance for factory premises	▼
Water used by production plant	▼
Labour cost of transferring materials between stores	▼

Picklist:

Allocate to administration overheads

Capitalise and depreciate over useful life

Direct cost

Charge to production in a machine hour overhead rate

Activity based charge to products

....

Task 1e

Select the appropriate term to match each of these descriptions.

Description	Term
A method of costing which allocates overheads to cost units by considering the activities that cause the overhead to be incurred and the factors that give rise to the costs (cost drivers)	▼
A method of costing which includes all production overheads within the cost of the cost units	▼
A method of costing which allocates overheads to cost units so that only the variable costs (or marginal costs) of production are included in the cost per cost unit	▼
The factor that causes the costs for each cost pool	▼

Picklist:

Absorption costing

Variable or marginal costing

Cost driver

Activity based costing

....

Task 2a

Complete the following production forecast for product J based on the information below. Do not show decimals. Round any decimal figures *up to the next whole number* of units.

Closing inventory is expected to be 10% more than opening inventory for each month.

Production (units)	July	August	September
Sales	1,000	1,000	1,000
Opening inventory	500		
Closing inventory			
Production			
Sub-total			

Task 2b

Calculate production and inventory levels.

Do not show decimals. Round any decimal figures *up to the next whole number* of litres.

50 workers are each expected to work 1,800 hours a year basic time.

10% of this time is idle time.

Each unit requires 15 minutes of labour time

3% of units are rejected as defective.

The opening inventory will be 50,263 units.

How many non-defective units will be produced?   units

How many units will be in inventory at the end of the period?   units

Task 2c

Calculate materials usage.

The sales budget is for 200,000 units in the period.

Each unit requires 3kg of material.

The opening inventory is 18,000 units.

The closing inventory is 35,000 units.

What is the materials usage budget? [   ] **kg**

Task 2d

Calculate materials usage.

Product A contains 5kg of material X.

1,000 units of product A are to be produced.

Product B contains 2kg of material X.

2,000 units of product B are to be produced.

Product C contains 1kg of material X.

500 units of product C are to be produced.
The production process for each product wastes 2% of material.

What is the materials usage budget (rounded to the nearest kg)? [   ] kg

Task 3a

Operating budget

Enter the missing figures in the working schedules and operating budget using the data from the production budget and the notes below.

Production budget	Units
Opening inventory of finished goods	5,000
Production	42,000
Sub-total	47,000
Sales	44,000
Closing inventory of finished goods	3,000

Complete these three working schedules.

Materials

Each unit produced requires 1.2kg of material.

Closing inventory will be valued at the budgeted purchase price.

Materials	Kg	£
Opening inventory	7,200	10,080
Purchases	49,200	73,800
Sub-total	56,400	83,880
Used in production		
Closing inventory		

Labour

It takes 6 minutes to make each item.

22 staff work 180 basic hours each.

Overtime is paid at 40% above the basic hourly rate.

Labour	Hours	£
Basic time @ £12 per hour		
Overtime		
Total		

Overhead

Variable overhead is recovered on total labour hours.

Overhead	Hours	£
Variable @ £1.10 per hour		
Fixed		3,348
Total		

Task 3b

Now complete the operating budget.

Enter income, costs and inventories as positive figures.

Closing inventory will be valued at the budgeted total cost of production per unit.

Use a negative figure to indicate a gross loss, for example –500 or (500).

Use a negative figure to indicate an operating loss, for example –500 or (500).

Operating budget	Units	£ per unit	£
Sales revenue		4.20	
Cost of goods sold:			
Opening inventory of finished goods			15,000
Cost of production		£	
Materials			
Labour			
Overhead			
Closing inventory of finished goods			
Cost of goods sold			
Gross profit			
Overheads:		£	
Administration		1,500	
Marketing		2,100	
Operating profit			

Task 4a

Stratified sampling

Calculate the number of customers to be interviewed from each geographical region to obtain a representative response from 2,300 interviews.

Do not show decimals. Round to the nearest whole number.

	North	South	East	West	Total
Number of customers	25,000	30,000	11,000	52,000	
Sample					

Task 4b

Break a budget down into accounting periods

Calculate the sales revenue and cost budgets for January using the budgeted unit data and the information below.

Do not show decimals. Round to the nearest whole number.

- Material costs are variable.
- The company has 25 workers working equal basic hours each month, totalling 2,000 per worker in the year.
- Labour costs £9 per hour basic time. Overtime is paid at £11 per hour.
- Each unit requires 0.5 hours of labour.
- Administrative costs are incurred evenly through the year.

Budgeted units	Year	January
Units sold	100,000	8,333
Units produced	105,000	9,000

Budget in £	Year	January
Sales revenue	5,000,000	
Material used	472,500	
Direct labour	477,500	
Administrative expenditure	24,000	

Task 4c

Cash flow forecast

Prepare the forecast from the operating budget and statement of financial position (balance sheet) assumptions.

Enter receipts and payments as positive figures.

Statement of financial position (balance sheet) assumptions:

- Receivables will decrease by £5,000.

- Materials payables will increase by £5,300.

- Labour are paid one month in arrears. This month's labour cost is 2% higher than that of the previous month.

- Other payables will increase by £2,100.

Operating budget	£	£
Sales revenue		96,000
Expenditure:		
Materials	21,500	
Labour	51,000	
Other costs	19,800	94,000
Operating profit		2,000

Cash flow forecast (to be completed)	£	£
Sales receipts		
Payments:		
Materials		
Labour		
Other costs		
Cash flow		

Task 5

You have prepared a draft direct labour budget for the coming year.

Background information

An organisation provides training for students wishing to pass professional examinations. The organisation offers a 'guaranteed pass' scheme, to which the following data relates.

Data collected includes:

- Number of courses
- Number of students
- Number of qualifications awarded

Draft direct labour budget	This year Actual	Next year Budget
Number of courses	2,567	2,465
Number of students	56,474	58,062
Number of qualifications awarded	9,412	9,677
Labour hours per qualification awarded	87	83
Labour		
Required for production (hours)	818,844	803,250
Labour hours @ Standard rate	750,000	750,000
Labour cost @ Standard rate (£20/hour)	£15,000,000	£14,000,000
Labour hours @ Overtime rate	68,844	53,250
Labour cost @ Overtime rate (£30/hour)	£2,065,320	£1,597,250
Direct labour cost total (£)	**£17,065,320**	**£15,597,250**

Write an e-mail to the budget committee, in 2 parts:

(a) **Requesting approval for the budget and explaining the assumptions upon which it is based.**

(b) **Recommending four performance indicators that could be used to measure the quality of the organisation's service, against budget. You are not restricted to using only the data listed above.**

| To | Budget committee | **Date** | xxxxx |
| **From** | An Accounting Technician | **Subject** | Performance indicators for quality |

(a)   Budget submission

(b)   Performance indicators for quality

Task 6a

Budget revision

You have submitted a draft operating budget to the budget committee. The committee has asked you to budget for an alternative scenario and calculate the increase or decrease in expected profit.

Complete the alternative scenario column in the operating budget table and calculate the increase or decrease in profit.

Assumptions in the first scenario

Material and labour costs are variable.

Depreciation is a stepped cost, increasing at every 6,500 units.

There is an allowance for a water price rise of 4%.

Alternative scenario

Increase the selling price by 9%.

Reduce the sales volume by 9%.

Revise the water price rise to 5%.

Apart from sales price per unit, do not enter decimals.

Round to the nearest whole number, if necessary.

Operating budget	First draft	Alternative scenario
Sales price £ per unit	6.00	
Sales volume	90,000	
	£	£
Sales revenue	540,000	
Costs:		
Materials	190,000	
Labour	150,500	
Water	16,666	
Depreciation	7,000	
Total	362,466	
Gross profit	177,534	
Increase/(decrease) in gross profit		

Task 6b

Variance analysis

Prepare the direct materials cost statement from the activity data provided

Enter favourable variances as positive figures – for example 500.

Enter adverse variances as negative figures – for example –500.

Activity data	Items produced	Materials used (kg)	Cost (£)
Budget	2,000	44,000	880,000
Actual results	2,420	45,980	827,640

Direct materials cost statement	£
Standard direct materials cost of production	
Variances (adverse shown as negative)	
Materials price	
Materials usage	
Materials cost	

Task 7

Monthly operating report

The budgeted and actual performance for a month is given below.

Flex the budget to the actual activity level, given the information below about costs, and show whether each variance is favourable or adverse.

Enter favourable variances as positive figures – for example 500.

Enter adverse variances as negative figures – for example –500.

Operating budget		Flexed budget	Actual	Variance Fav/(Adv)
120,000	Sales volume (units)		140,000	
£		£	£	£
6,000,000	Sales revenue		6,720,000	
	Costs			
1,080,000	Material		1,313,680	
660,000	Labour		782,310	
150,000	Production managers		192,000	
24,000	Distribution		35,281	
250,000	Energy		296,530	
414,000	Depreciation		412,000	
332,000	Marketing and advertising		315,320	
529,000	Administration		534,200	
3,439,000	Total costs		3,881,321	
2,561,000	Operating profit		2,838,679	

Material, labour and distribution costs are variable.

Energy cost is semi-variable. The variable element is budgeted at £1.50 per unit of sales.

Production managers are a stepped cost. For health and safety reasons, there must always be at least two production managers for each production line in operation. Each production line has a maximum output of 45,000 units per month and only the minimum number of production lines are operated each month.

Depreciation, marketing and advertising, and administration costs are fixed.

You are required to flex the budget, calculate variances and show whether each variance is favourable or adverse. The actual results have been entered for you.

Task 8

Operational review

Review the operating statement shown and the additional information below, and prepare a report by email.

Additional information

The business manufactures chocolates.

During the period, the world's largest supplier of the raw material, cocoa, purchased a competitor and was able to push prices upwards given its large market share. The business switched suppliers several times, but this led to quality issues.

During the summer, one of the two machines for production broke down. This led to the machine being out of service for two weeks while a specialist carried out extensive repairs.

Following the decision to stop giving inventory away free to staff, the workforce slowed their production for three weeks until management reversed its decision.

Operating statement	Flexed budget	Actual	Variance Fav/(Adverse)
	£	£	£
Sales revenue	12,400,000	11,000,000	(1,400,000)
Material	(2,550,000)	(4,012,500)	(1,462,500)
Labour	(5,350,000)	(5,800,000)	(450,000)
Variable production overheads	(1,070,000)	(1,085,000)	(15,000)
Fixed production overheads	(535,000)	(791,250)	(256,250)
Profit/(loss)	2,895,000	(688,750)	(3,583,750)

Write an email to the Managing Director in which you:

(a) **Suggest possible reasons for the variances on materials, labour, fixed production overheads and sales.**

(b) **Explain actions that should be taken in relation to setting the following year's budget, in the light of these variances.**

To	Managing Director	Date	(Today)
From	Budget Accountant	Subject	Reasons for variances and actions

Reasons for variances

Actions

BPP PRACTICE ASSESSMENT 2
BUDGETING

ANSWERS

Task 1a

Overheads	Method of allocation
Rent and rates	Number of staff employed
Canteen expenses	Floor area
Inventory insurance	Units produced
	Average inventory held

Task 1b

As budget accountant, match each task with the person or group that you will need to contact.

(CBT instructions: Click on a box in the left column, then on one in the right column. To remove a line, click on it.)

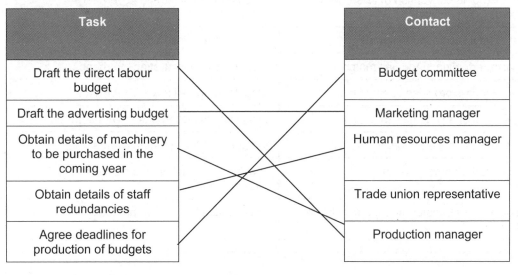

Task	Contact
Draft the direct labour budget	Budget committee
Draft the advertising budget	Marketing manager
Obtain details of machinery to be purchased in the coming year	Human resources manager
Obtain details of staff redundancies	Trade union representative
Agree deadlines for production of budgets	Production manager

Task 1c

Classification	Expenditure
Labour	
Material	Wastage costs incurred on production line
Sales and marketing	Advertising costs
Administration	Legal fees regarding late payment by customers
	Depreciation costs of new computer system
	Cost of annual audit
Capital	Cost of new computer system for office

Task 1d

Cost	Accounting treatment
Purchase of latest version of IT software package	Allocate to administration overheads
Cost of new marketing materials	Allocate to administration overheads
Client entertaining at football match	Allocate to administration overheads
Company cars provided to sales team	Allocate to administration overheads
Legal costs of buying new factory	Capitalise and depreciate over useful life
Buildings insurance for factory premises	Allocate to administration overheads
Water used by production plant	Charge to production in a machine hour overhead rate
Labour cost of transferring materials between stores	Activity based charge to products

Task 1e

Description	Term
A method of costing which allocates overheads to cost units by considering the activities that cause the overhead to be incurred and the factors that give rise to the costs (cost drivers)	Activity based costing
A method of costing which includes all production overheads within the cost of the cost units	Absorption costing
A method of costing which allocates overheads to cost units so that only the variable costs (or marginal costs) of production are included in the cost per cost unit	Variable or marginal costing
The factor that causes the costs for each cost pool	Cost driver

Task 2a

	July	August	September
Sales	1,000	1,000	1,000
Opening inventory	500	550	605
Closing inventory	550	605	666
Production	1,050	1,055	1,061
Sub-total	1,550	1,605	1,666

Task 2b

The correct answers are: **314,280** and **364,543**

Working

Hours worked = 50 × 1,800 = 90,000

Productive hours = 90,000 × 90% = 81,000 hours

Hours per unit = 0.25

Units produced = 81,000/0.25 = 324,000

Non-defective units produced = 97% × 324,000 = 314,280

Opening inventory = 50,263

Closing inventory = 50,263 + 314,280 = 364,543

Task 2c

The materials usage budget is | 651,000 | kg

Working

Production budget = sales + closing inventory – opening inventory = 200,000 + 35,000 – 18,000 = 217,000 units.

Materials usage = 217,000 × 3kg = 651,000 kg

Task 2d

The materials usage budget in kg is | 9,694 |

Working

Material required:

Product A: 5kg × 1,000 = 5,000 kg

Product B: 2kg × 2,000 = 4,000 kg

Product C: 1kg × 500 = 500kg

Total = 9,500kg

Total including wastage = 9,500 × 100/98 = 9,694 kg

Task 3a

Materials	kg	£
Opening inventory	7,200	10,080
Purchases	49,200	73,800
Sub-total	56,400	83,880
Used in production	50,400	74,880
Closing inventory	6,000	9,000

Working

42,000 × 1.2kg = 50,400 kg will be used in production, leaving 56,400 − 50,400 = 6,000 kgs in inventory. These are valued at £73,800/£49,200 = £1.50 each, that is at £9,000. The cost of material used in production is therefore £83,880 − £9,000 = £74,880.

Labour	Hours	£
Basic time @ £12 per hour	3,960	47,520
Overtime	240	4,032
Total	4,200	51,552

Working

42,000 × 6/60 = 4,200 labour hours are required in total but only 22 × 180 = 3,960 basic hours are available, so 4,200 − 3,960 = 240 hours must be paid at overtime rates: 240 × £12 × 1.4 = £4,032.

Overhead	Hours	£
Variable @ £1.10 per hour	4,200	4,620
Fixed		3,348
Total		7,968

Task 3b

Operating budget	Units	£ per unit	£
Sales revenue	44,000	4.20	184,800
Cost of goods sold:			
Opening inventory of finished goods			15,000
Cost of production		£	
Materials		74,880	
Labour		51,552	
Overhead		7,968	134,400
Closing inventory of finished goods (134,400/42,000 3,000)			9,600
Cost of goods sold			139,800
Gross profit			45,000
Overheads			
Administration		1,500	
Marketing		2,100	3,600
Operating profit			41,400

Task 4a

	North	South	East	West	Total
Number of customers	25,000	30,000	11,000	52,000	118,000
Sample	487	585	214	1,014	2,300

Workings

North	25,000 / 118,000 × 2,300	487
South	30,000 / 118,000 × 2,300	585
East	11,000 / 118,000 × 2,300	214
West	52,000 / 118,000 × 2,300	1,014

Task 4b

Budgeted units	Year	January
Units sold	100,000	8,333
Units produced	105,000	9,000

	Year	January
Sales revenue	5,000,000	416,650 W1
Material used	472,500	40,500 W2
Direct labour	477,500	41,166 W3
Administrative expenditure	24,000	2,000

Workings

1. Sales price per unit = £5,000,000/100,000 = £50

    January sales = 8,333 × £50 = £416,650

2. Material

    Price per unit = £472,500/105,000 = £4.50 per unit

    January materials usage = £4.5 × 9,000 = £40,500

3. Labour

    Labour hours needed for January = 9,000 × 0.5 = 4,500

    Labour hours available = 2,000 × 25/12 = 4,167

    Labour cost = (4,167 × £9) + ((4,500 − 4,167) × £11) = £41,166

Task 4c

Operating budget	£	£
Sales revenue		96,000
Expenditure:		
Materials	21,500	
Labour	51,000	
Other costs	19,800	94,000
Operating profit		2,000

Cash flow forecast (to be completed)	£	£
Sales receipts		101,000
Payments:		
Materials	16,200	
Labour *	50,000	
Other costs	17,700	83,900
Cash flow		17,100

* Labour cost = 51,000 ÷ 1.02 = 50,000.

Task 5

To	Budget committee	Date	xxxxx
From	An Accounting Technician	Subject	Performance indicators for quality

(a)   Budget submission

I attach the proposed labour budget for next year for your consideration and approval. This year's results are shown for comparison.

This draft is based on the agreed number of 2,465 courses, which is 4% fewer than this year. The total number of labour hours is expected to fall from 818,844 to 803,250, which is 2%.

The number of labour hours worked at the Standard rate will remain constant at 750,000 hours. The fall in the total labour hours needed will result in a fall in overtime hours from 68,844 hours to 53,250 hours. Overtime payments will fall by £468,070.

Overall the direct labour budget shows a reduction of 8.6% compared with this year. However, the number of qualifications awarded is set to rise by 2.8%, which should result in increased revenue being recognised during the year.

(b)   Performance indicators for quality

A number of different indicators can help assess quality. Standards or targets must be set and then the actual performance compared against these.

Many quantitative indicators are given below. However, as the quality of service will also be judged by the students i.e. the customers, I recommend surveys are undertaken at the end of each course to obtain feedback about the quality of service from the students.

Non-financial quantitative indicators:

Percentage of students awarded a qualification

Number of individual exam passes

Number of first time passes per number of exams taken

Pass rates per course

Number of complaints from students

Average marks obtained compared with average for that exam nationwide

Tutorial note: only four indicators are required.

Task 6a

Operating budget	First draft	Alternative scenario	Working
Sales price £ per unit	6.00	6.54	*6 × 1.09*
Sales volume	90,000	81,900	*90,000 × 0.91*
	£	£	
Sales revenue	540,000	535,626	*6.54 × 81,900*
Costs:			
Materials	190,000	172,900	*190,000 × 0.91*
Labour	150,500	136,955	*150,500 × 0.91*
Energy	16,666	16,826	*16,666/1.04 × 1.05*
Depreciation	7,000	6,500	*W1*
Total	362,466	333,181	
Gross profit	177,534	202,445	
Increase/(decrease) in gross profit		24,911	

Workings

W1

Depreciation is in steps of 6,500 by volume. Therefore the charge at volume of 90,000 puts this at the 14th step. Each step is therefore £7,000 ÷ 14 = £500.

A volume of 81,900 ÷ 6,500 = 12.6, ie the 13th step. £500 × 13 = £6,500.

....

Task 6b

Direct materials cost statement	£
Standard direct materials cost of production	1,064,800 *W1*
Materials price	91,960 *W2*
Materials usage	145,200 *W3*
Materials cost	237,160

Workings

W1

880,000 ÷ 2,000 = £440

£440 × 2,420 = £1,064,800

W2

Standard price = 880,000 ÷ 44,000 = £20/kg

Actual price = 827,640 ÷ 45,980 = £18/kg

Materials price variance = (£20 – £18) × 45,980 = £91,960

Variance is favourable – price is lower than budget.

W3

Standard usage = 44,000 ÷ 2,000 = 22kg/unit

Actual usage = 45,980 ÷ 2,420 = 19kg/unit

Materials usage variance = (22 – 19) × £20/kg × 2,420 = £145,200

Variance is favourable – usage is lower than budget (fewer kgs per unit).

Task 7

Operating budget		Flexed budget	Actual	Variance Fav/(Adv)
120,000	Sales volume (units)		140,000	
£		£	£	£
6,000,000	Sales revenue	7,000,000	6,720,000	−280,000
	Costs			
1,080,000	Material	1,260,000	1,313,680	−53,680
660,000	Labour	770,000	782,310	−12,310
150,000	Production managers	200,000	192,000	8,000
24,000	Distribution	28,000	35,281	−7,281
250,000	Energy	280,000	296,530	−16,530
414,000	Depreciation	414,000	412,000	2,000
332,000	Marketing and advertising	332,000	315,320	16,680
529,000	Administration	529,000	534,200	−5,200
3,439,000	Total costs	3,813,000	3,881,321	−68,321
2,561,000	Operating profit	3,187,000	2,838,679	−348,321

Working

1. Sales £6,000,000/120,000 = £50 per unit, so flexed budget is 140,000 × £50 = £7,000,000

2. Materials £1,080,000/120,000 = £9 per unit, so flexed budget is 140,000 × £9 = £1,260,000

3. Labour £660,000/120,000 = £5.50 per unit, so flexed budget is 140,000 × £5.50 = £770,000

4. Production managers: 120,000/45,000 = 2.67, so 3 production lines were budgeted to be in operation requiring 2 production managers each. This is six in total at £150,000/6 = £25,000 each. When production is 140,000 units, 140,000/45,000 = 3.11 ie 4 production lines in operation and 8 production managers are needed, at a cost of 8 × £25,000 = £200,000.

5. Distribution £24,000/120,000 = £0.20/unit. Flexed budget: 140,000 × £0.20 = £28,000

6. Energy variable element: 120,000 × £1.50 = £180,000, so fixed element is £250,000 − £180,000 = £70,000. Therefore flexed budget this year is (140,000 × £1.50) + £70,000 = £280,000

Task 8

To	Managing Director	Date	(Today)
From	Budget Accountant	Subject	Reasons for variances and actions

Reasons for variances

Sales variance

As the budget has been flexed, prices were lower than expected per unit. This may have reflected discounting if the brand image had suffered due to quality issues.

Materials variance

There is an adverse materials variance due to the increase in prices by the key supplier. Our attempt to source cocoa from alternative suppliers led to quality problems and so we used more cocoa than expected (adverse usage variance in addition to adverse price variance).

Labour variance

This was partly due to the machine breakdown, when staff were unable to work, but also due to the staff unrest because of the stoppage of free chocolate to staff. Staff were therefore both paid for work when they were idle, and were less efficient because they were less motivated.

Fixed production overheads

The use of specialist engineers to fix the machinery will have contributed to the adverse fixed overheads variance.

Actions

If we cannot source a reliable, cheaper supplier of cocoa then the standard cost of material should be increased in the next budget, to reflect the prices charged by the key supplier.

No amendment should be made to the standards used in the budget in relation to labour, as both occurrences (staff go-slow and machine breakdown) are hopefully not to be repeated.

If not, for example if the breakdown is indicative of the machinery becoming less reliable, it may be necessary to budget for higher maintenance costs within fixed production overheads in future.

If we have had to reduce prices permanently because of image problems, we should amend the standard selling price in the next budget.

BPP PRACTICE ASSESSMENT 3
BUDGETING

Time allowed: 2.5 hours

Task 1a

Match the information with an appropriate source which will provide, or help you forecast, that information when constructing a budget.

(CBT instructions: Click on a box in the left column, then on one in the right column. To remove a line, click on it.)

Information required
Foreign exchange rates
National Insurance Contribution rates
Interest rates on factory mortgage
Sales demand of a new product
Irrecoverable debts
Directors' bonuses

Source
Market research consultant
HM Revenue & Customs website
Credit controller
Loan agreement
Articles of Association of Company
Board minutes
The Financial Times

Task 1b

Who would you contact in each of the following situations? *(CBT instructions: Click on a box in the left column, then on one in the right column. To remove a line, click on it.)*

Situation
You want to explain a materials usage variance
You want your budget to be authorised
You want to explain a materials purchases variance

Pick from
Purchasing department
Managing director
Sales department
Budget committee
Production manager

Task 1c

Select the appropriate budget for the following items of expenditure:

Expenditure	Budget
Annual service cost of equipment	▼
Depreciation of printer used to produce marketing brochures	▼
Fuel costs for delivery trucks	▼
Purchase of new delivery truck	▼
Depreciation of delivery truck	▼

Picklist:

- Distribution budget
- Marketing budget
- Repairs and maintenance budget
- Capital budget

Task 1d

Select an appropriate accounting treatment for each of the following costs:

Expenditure	Accounting treatment
Material wastage	▼
Companies House penalty for late filing	▼
Food and drink at opening of new showroom	▼
Cost of purchasing manager	▼
Room hire for office staff training course	▼
Material storage costs	▼
Machinery maintenance costs	▼

Picklist:

- Activity-based charge to production cost centres
- Allocate to marketing overheads
- Allocate to administrative overheads
- Charge to production at a machine hour overhead rate
- Direct cost

Task 1e

Select the appropriate term to match each of these descriptions.

Description	Term
An area of the business which incurs costs, but also generates income	▼
A costing method which includes all production overheads within the cost of the cost units	▼
An area of the business with costs and revenues which also accounts for its own capital employed	▼
A costing method which includes only variable costs within the cost of the cost units with fixed costs written off as period costs	▼

Picklist:

Profit centre
Investment centre
Absorption costing
Marginal costing

Task 2a

Closing inventory is to be 20% of the next period's sales. Sales in period 4 will be 12,000 units.

Complete the following production budget in units for the product.

	Period 1	Period 2	Period 3
Opening inventory	2,200		
Production			
Subtotal			
Sales	11,000	11,500	11,700
Closing inventory			

Task 2b

The next three months' production budget is shown below. Of the completed units, 2% fail a quality test and are scrapped.

How many units must be manufactured to allow for the scrapped units?

	Month 1	Month 2	Month 3
Required units	18,000	20,000	15,000
Manufactured units			

Task 2c

A product uses a material P in its production. P costs £3 per litre. The materials purchasing budget for material P in the next quarter is being constructed. The budgeted production is 5,000 units in the next quarter.

Each unit of product uses 0.75 litres of P, but a further 0.05 litres is lost in wastage for every unit made. There will be inventory levels of 345 litres of P at the start of the quarter, but inventory of only 150 litres is required at the end of the quarter.

What is the materials purchasing budget (in £) for the coming next quarter?

Select from:

- £3,805
- £4,195
- £11,415
- £12,585

Task 2d

A company makes two products, A and B, using the same grade of labour. The company pays 10 employees for a 35 hour week, regardless of whether all hours are worked, at a rate of £10 per hour. Overtime is paid at £12 per hour.

Product A requires 0.5 labour hours

Product B requires 2 labour hours

The budgeted production for the next four week period is

Product A   500 units

Product B   500 units

What is the labour cost budget for the next four week period?

Select from:

- £12,500
- £12,600
- £14,000
- £16,100

Task 3a

You are required to complete the following working schedules and operating budget for production of 16,000 units.

Working schedules

Materials

	Kg	£
Opening inventory	500	1,000
Purchases	2,400	6,000
Sub-total	2,900	7,000
Usage		
Closing inventory	450	

Closing inventory of raw material is to be valued at budgeted purchase price

Labour

	Hours	£
Basic time @ £15 per hour		
Overtime		
Total		

Each unit takes 6 minutes. There are 1,400 basic labour hours available. Overtime is paid at time and a half

Overhead

	Hours	£
Variable @ £0.80 per hour		
Fixed		4,000
Total		

Variable overhead recovered on total labour hours

BPP
LEARNING MEDIA

Task 3b

Operating budget

	Units	£
Sales @ £2.40 each	15,000	
Opening inventory	–	
Cost of production	16,000	
Materials		
Labour		
Overhead		
Total production cost		
Closing inventory of finished goods	1,000	
Cost of goods sold		
Gross profit		

Closing inventory of finished goods is valued at budgeted production cost per unit.

∙∙∙

Task 4a

Last year sales were £4,000,000.

Analysis of recent years shows a growth trend of 8% per annum.

The seasonal variation has been:

Quarter	£
Quarter 1	−£10,000
Quarter 2	+£25,000
Quarter 3	+£35,000
Quarter 4	−£50,000

Forecast the income for each quarter of the coming year.

Quarter	£
Quarter 1	
Quarter 2	
Quarter 3	
Quarter 4	
Year	

Task 4b

The following budget has been constructed for a year.

	Budget for the year	Budget for month 1
Sales forecast (units)	200,000	16,000
Production budget (units)	180,000	14,000
	£	£
Sales	900,000	
Materials used	270,000	
Labour	36,000	
Variable production overhead	180,000	
Variable selling overhead	100,000	
Fixed overheads	58,000	

Material, labour and variable production overheads are variable with the number of units produced.

Variable selling overheads vary with units sold.

Fixed overheads are incurred evenly throughout the year.

Complete the budget for month 1.

....

Task 4c

Cash flow forecast

Prepare the forecast from the operating budget and statement of financial position (balance sheet) assumptions.

Enter receipts and payments as positive figures.

Statement of financial position (balance sheet) assumptions:

- Receivables will increase by £2,500.
- Materials payables will increase by £1,750.
- Labour costs are paid in the period in which they are incurred.
- Other payables will reduce by £3,400.

Operating budget	£	£
Sales revenue		115,000
Expenditure:		
Materials	32,150	
Labour	41,300	
Other costs	12,300	85,750
Operating profit		29,250

Cash flow forecast (to be completed)	£	£
Sales receipts		
Payments:		
Materials		
Labour		
Other costs		
Cash flow		

....

Task 5

You have been responsible for preparing a cash budget. An extract is given below showing cash inflows.

Cash budget

	This year's actual cash inflows £	Next year £
Cash inflows from sales	185,000	179,000
Proceeds from sale of car		14,000

You have constructed the budget with reference to this year's cash inflows and the following information.

Sales are expected to remain constant. Receivables at the end of this year are £30,000. Historically, year end receivables are kept at this level but they are expected to increase by 20% by the end of next year.

The managing director's car is sold every two years at a loss of around £10,000, and replaced with a better model.

The managing director is concerned that sales appear to be decreasing in this cash budget, and asks for an explanation regarding the car sale.

Write an email to the Managing Director explaining the calculations and assumptions in your cash budget. Address his concern regarding sales and the car transaction.

To	Managing Director	Date	(Today)
From	Budget Accountant	Subject	Cash Budget inflows

Sales

Car

Task 6a

Budget revision

You have submitted a draft operating budget to the budget committee. The committee has asked you to budget for an alternative scenario and calculate the increase or decrease in expected profit.

Complete the alternative scenario column in the operating budget table and calculate the increase or decrease in profit.

Assumptions in the first scenario

Material and labour costs are variable.

Depreciation is a stepped cost, increasing at every 7,000 units.

There is an allowance for an energy price rise of 5%.

Alternative scenario

Increase the selling price by 4%.

Reduce the sales volume by 12%.

Revise the energy price rise to 3%.

Apart from sales price per unit, do not enter decimals.

Round to the nearest whole number, if necessary.

Operating budget	First draft	Alternative scenario
Sales price £ per unit	12.00	
Sales volume	50,000	
	£	£
Sales revenue	600,000	
Costs:		
Materials	212,500	
Labour	202,250	
Energy	16,275	
Depreciation	9,600	
Total	440,625	
Gross profit	159,375	
Increase/(decrease) in gross profit		

Task 6b

Variance analysis

Prepare the direct labour cost statement from the activity data provided

Enter favourable variances as positive figures – for example 500.

Enter adverse variances as negative figures – for example –500.

Activity data	Items produced	Labour hours	Cost (£)
Budget	48,000	372,000	2,604,000
Actual results	50,000	385,000	2,810,500

Direct labour cost statement	£
Standard direct labour cost of production	
Variances (adverse shown as negative)	
Labour rate	
Labour efficiency	
Labour cost	

Task 7

The budgeted and actual performance for a month is given below.

Flex the budget to the actual activity level, given the information below about costs, and show whether each variance is favourable or adverse.

	Budget	Flexed budget	Actual	Variance Fav/(Adv)
Sales volume	100,000	120,000	120,000	
	£	£	£	£
Sales revenue	4,500,000		4,865,000	
Material	2,200,000		2,437,500	
Labour	500,000		518,000	
Light, heat, power	72,000		90,000	
Depreciation	100,000		90,000	
Administration	220,000		230,000	
Marketing	180,000		190,000	
Profit	1,228,000		1,309,500	

Material and labour costs are variable.

The cost for light, heat and power is semi-variable. The budgeted fixed element is £22,000.

The budget for marketing costs is stepped, increasing every 80,000 units.

Depreciation and administration costs are fixed.

....

Task 8

You are asked to review the operating statement shown below, and the background information provided, and to make recommendations.

Operating statement for the year ended 30 June 20X6

	Budget £	Actual £	Variance Fav/(adv)
Sales revenue	3,450,000	3,260,000	(190,000)
Variable costs			
Material	1,090,000	1,092,000	(2,000)
Labour	540,000	590,000	(50,000)
Fixed costs			
Marketing & PR	450,000	250,000	200,000
Depreciation	150,000	149,000	1,000
Administration	260,000	254,000	6,000
	960,000	925,000	(35,000)

The budget has been flexed to reflect the actual number of units produced and sold in the year. The original budget had been prepared at the start of the year and no further revisions had been made.

The sales and marketing director was dismissed during the year, as he was found to have been using company marketing funds for personal entertaining. No replacement has yet been found for the director.

The departure of the sales and marketing director led to the cancellation of a large advertising campaign that he had planned for the coming year. The Managing Director temporarily oversaw the marketing team and decided that a reduction in sales price would be just as effective as a large marketing campaign.

Due to cash flow problems during the year, the company lost a prompt payment discount for one of its main materials. A new bonus initiative for production workers was introduced to discourage materials wastage.

The Managing Director is confused about what the variances mean in terms of the eventful year that the company has had.

Write an email to the Managing Director suggesting possible reasons for the major variances, and advising on any action that should be taken with respect to the standards used when setting the budget for the next year.

To	Managing Director	Date	(Today)
From	Budget Accountant	Subject	Variances for the year ended 30 June 20X6

Variances and action to be taken

BPP PRACTICE ASSESSMENT 3
BUDGETING

ANSWERS

Task 1a

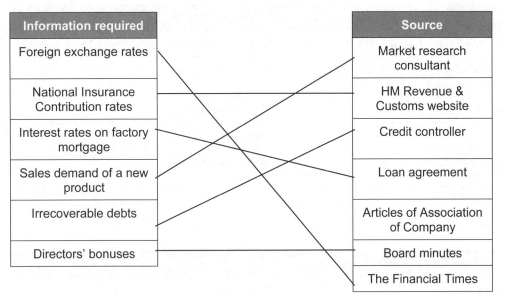

Information required	Source
Foreign exchange rates	Market research consultant
National Insurance Contribution rates	HM Revenue & Customs website
Interest rates on factory mortgage	Credit controller
Sales demand of a new product	Loan agreement
Irrecoverable debts	Articles of Association of Company
Directors' bonuses	Board minutes
	The Financial Times

Task 1b

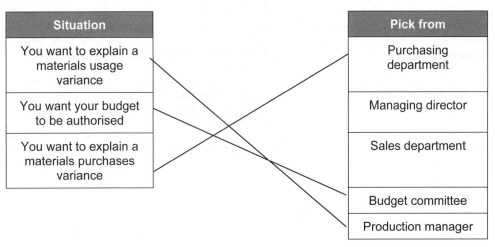

Situation	Pick from
You want to explain a materials usage variance	Purchasing department
You want your budget to be authorised	Managing director
You want to explain a materials purchases variance	Sales department
	Budget committee
	Production manager

Task 1c

Expenditure	Budget
Annual service cost of equipment	Repairs and maintenance budget
Depreciation of printer used to produce marketing brochures	Marketing budget
Fuel costs for delivery trucks	Distribution budget
Purchase of new delivery truck	Capital budget
Depreciation of delivery truck	Distribution budget

Task 1d

Expenditure	Accounting treatment
Material wastage	Direct cost
Companies House penalty for late filing	Allocate to administrative overheads
Food and drink at opening of new showroom	Allocate to marketing overheads
Cost of purchasing manager	Activity-based charge to production cost centres
Room hire for office staff training course	Allocate to administrative overheads
Material storage costs	Activity-based charge to production cost centres
Machinery maintenance costs	Charge to production at a machine hour overhead rate. (Or – activity-based charge to production cost centres)

Task 1e

Description	Term
An area of the business which incurs costs, but also generates income	Profit centre
A costing method which includes all production overheads within the cost of the cost units	Absorption costing
An area of the business with costs and revenues which also accounts for its own capital employed	Investment centre
A costing method which includes only variable costs within the cost of the cost units with fixed costs written off as period costs	Marginal costing

Task 2a

	Period 1	Period 2	Period 3
Opening inventory	2,200	2,300	2,340
Production	11,100	11,540	11,760
Subtotal	13,300	13,840	14,100
Sales	11,000	11,500	11,700
Closing inventory	2,300	2,340	2,400

Workings

Closing inventory:

$20\% \times 11,500 = 2,300$

$20\% \times 11,700 = 2,340$

$20\% \times 12,000 = 2,400$

Production = sales + closing inventory − opening inventory

Period 1 production = 11,000 + 2,300 − 2,200 = 11,100

Period 2 production = 11,500 + 2,340 − 2,300 = 11,540

Period 3 production = 11,700 + 2,400 − 2,340 = 11,760

Task 2b

	Month 1	Month 2	Month 3
Required units	18,000	20,000	15,000
Manufactured units	18,368	20,409	15,307

Workings

$18,000 \times 100/98 = 18,368$ etc − must be rounded up to ensure sufficient units are made after 2% are scrapped.

Task 2c

The correct answer is **£11,415**

Workings

Material usage = budgeted production × budgeted usage per unit (including wastage)

= 5,000 × (0.75 + 0.05)

= 4,000 litres

Materials purchases (litres) = closing inventory + usage − opening inventory

= 150 + 4,000 − 345

= 3,805 litres

Materials purchase (in £) = £3 × 3,805 = £11,415

Task 2d

The correct answer is **£14,000**

Workings

Labour hours required for budgeted production:

Product A 500 × 0.5 = 250 hours

Product B 500 × 2 = 1,000 hours

Total hours required = 250 + 1,000 = 1,250 hours.

Hours available without overtime = 10 × 35 × 4 = 1,400 hours

Therefore no overtime is required, but the company must pay for 1,400 hours at £10 per hour = £14,000

Task 3a

Working schedules
Materials

	Kg	£
Opening inventory	500	1,000
Purchases	2,400	6,000
Sub-total	2,900	7,000
Usage	2,450	5,875
Closing inventory (450 × £6,000/2,400)	450	1,125

Labour

	Hours	£
Basic time @ £15 per hour	1,400	21,000
Overtime	200	4,500
Total	1,600	25,500

Overhead

	Hours	£
Variable @ £0.80 per hour	1,600	1,280
Fixed		4,000
Total		5,280

Task 3b

Operating budget

	Units	£
Sales @ £2.40 each	15,000	36,000
Opening inventory	0	0
Cost of production	16,000	
Materials		5,875
Labour		25,500
Overhead		5,280
Total production cost		36,655
Closing inventory of finished goods	1,000	2,291
Cost of goods sold		34,364
Gross profit		1,636

Workings

Materials:

Usage = opening inventory + purchases – closing inventory = 2,450 kg

Cost of closing inventory = £6,000/2,400 × 450 = £1,125

Usage price is the balance of £7,000 – £1,125 = £5,875

Labour

Time for production = 16,000 × 6/60 = 1,600 hours, therefore 200 overtime hours are required.

1,400 @ £15 per hour = £21,000

200 @ £15 × 1.5 = £4,500

Overheads = £0.80 × 1,600 = £1,280

Closing inventory = total production cost/16,000 × 1,000 = £2,291

Deduct from total production cost to give cost of sales £36,655 – £2,291 = £34,364

Task 4a

Quarter	£
Quarter 1 (£1,080,000 − £10,000)	1,070,000
Quarter 2 (£1,080,000 + £25,000)	1,105,000
Quarter 3 (£1,080,000 + £35,000)	1,115,000
Quarter 4 (£1,080,000 − £50,000)	1,030,000
Year	4,320,000

Workings

Last year sales = £4,000,000

But trend is 8% growth = 1.08 × £4,000,000 = £4,320,000

Sales per quarter (trend) = £4,320,000/4 = £1,080,000

Task 4b

	Budget for the year	Budget for month 1
Sales forecast (units)	200,000	16,000
Production budget (units)	180,000	14,000
	£	£
Sales	900,000	72,000
Materials used	270,000	21,000
Labour	36,000	2,800
Variable production overhead	180,000	14,000
Variable selling overhead	100,000	8,000
Fixed overheads	58,000	4,833

Workings

1. Sales

    Sales price per unit = £900,000/200,000 = £4.50 per unit.

    Therefore, sales of 16,000 units = £4.50 × 16,000 = £72,000

2. Materials

    Materials cost per unit produced (using annual budget) = £270,000/180,000 = £1.50 per unit.

Material cost of 14,000 units in month 1 = 14,000 × £1.50 = £21,000

3. Labour

    Labour cost per unit produced (from annual budget) = £36,000/180,000 = £0.20

    Labour cost of 14,000 units in month 1 = 14,000 × £0.20 = £2,800

4. Variable production overhead

    Variable production overhead per unit (from annual budget) = £180,000/180,000 = £1.00 per unit

    Variable production overhead costs for month 1 = 14,000 × £1.00 = £14,000

5. Variable selling overheads

    Variable selling overheads per unit (from annual budget) = £100,000/200,000 = £0.50 per unit

    Variable selling overheads for month 1 = 16,000 × £0.50 = £8,000

6. Fixed overheads

    For month 1, fixed overhead = 58,000/12 = £4,833

Task 4c

Operating budget	£	£
Sales revenue		115,000
Expenditure:		
Materials	32,150	
Labour	41,300	
Other costs	12,300	85,750
Operating profit		29,250

Cash flow forecast	£	£
Sales receipts		112,500
Payments:		
Materials	30,400	
Labour	41,300	
Other costs	15,700	87,400
Cash flow		25,100

Task 5

> To   Managing Director   Date   (Today)
> From   Budget Accountant   Subject   Cash Budget inflows
>
> ---
>
> **Sales**
>
> I have prepared the cash budget by considering the change in receivable balances at the start and end of next year. Receivables are expected to increase by 20%, ie (£30,000 × 1.2) to £36,000. Sales are not decreasing but are expected to be the same as last year. However, as receivables will increase by £6,000 we will collect £6,000 less cash than the sales we actually make.
>
> Last year, there was no change in the receivables balance at the start and end of the year, so the cash collected from sales was therefore equal to those sales (£185,000).
>
> Assuming the same level of sales, and the £6,000 increase in receivables, means we will collect £185,000 − £6,000 = £179,000.
>
> ---
>
> **Car**
>
> We buy and sell a car for you every two years. The current carrying amount (net book value) of the car in the accounts is £24,000, but it is assumed that we will sell this for a £10,000 loss as in previous years, so the actual proceeds received will be £14,000 as shown in the cash budget.
>
> The extract you have is of the cash inflows only. You need to look at the full cash budget which will show the outflow of cash for the new car being purchased.

Task 6a

Operating budget	First draft	Alternative scenario	Working
Sales price £ per unit	12.00	12.48	*12 × 1.04*
Sales volume	50,000	44,000	*50,000 × 0.88*
	£	£	
Sales revenue	600,000	549,120	*12.48 × 44,000*
Costs:			
Materials	212,500	187,000	*212,500 × 0.88*
Labour	202,250	177,980	*202,250 × 0.88*
Energy	16,275	15,965	*16,275/1.05 × 1.03*
Depreciation	9,600	8,400	*W1*
Total	440,625	389,345	
Gross profit	159,375	159,775	
Increase/(decrease) in gross profit		400	

Workings

W1

Depreciation is in steps of 7,000 by volume. Therefore the charge at volume of 50,000 puts this at the 8th step. Each step is therefore £9,600 ÷ 8 = £1,200.

A volume of 44,000 ÷ 7,000 = 6.29, ie the 7th step. £1,200 × 7 = £8,400.

....

Task 6b

Direct labour cost statement	£
Standard direct labour cost of production	2,712,500 *W1*
Variances (adverse shown as negative)	
Labour rate	−115,500 *W2*
Labour efficiency	17,500 *W3*
Labour cost	−98,000

Workings

W1

2,604,000 ÷ 48,000 = £54.25

£54.25 × 50,000 = £2,712,500

W2

Standard rate = 2,604,000 ÷ 372,000 = £7.00/hr

Actual rate = 2,810,500 ÷ 385,000 = £7.30/hr

Labour rate variance = (£7 − £7.30) × 385,000 = −£115,500

Variance is adverse – rate is higher than budget.

W3

Standard efficiency = 372,000 ÷ 48,000 = 7.75hrs/unit

Actual efficiency = 385,000 ÷ 50,000 = 7.70hrs/unit

Labour efficiency variance = (7.75 − 7.70) × £7/hr × 50,000 = £17,500

Variance is favourable – efficiency is better than budget (fewer hours per unit).

Task 7

	Budget	Flexed budget	Actual	Variance
	100,000	120,000	120,000	
	£	£	£	£
Sales revenue (W1)	4,500,000	5,400,000	4,865,000	535,000A
Material (W2)	2,200,000	2,640,000	2,437,500	202,500F
Labour (W3)	500,000	600,000	518,000	82,000F
Light, heat, power (W4)	72,000	82,000	90,000	8,000A
Depreciation	100,000	100,000	90,000	10,000F
Administration	220,000	220,000	230,000	10,000A
Marketing (W5)	180,000	180,000	190,000	10,000A
Profit	1,228,000	1,578,000	1,309,500	268,500A

Workings

1. Budgeted selling price per unit

   Revenue/sales volume

   £4,500,000/100,000 = £45

   Flexed budget: 120,000 × £45 = £5,400,000

2. Budgeted material cost

   £2,200,000/100,000 = £22

   Flexed budget: 120,000 × £22 = £2,640,000

3. Budgeted labour cost

   £500,000/100,000 = £5

   Flexed budget: 120,000 × £5 = £600,000

4. Budgeted light, heat, power cost

   Fixed element = £22,000

   Original budget, variable element = £72,000 − £22,000 = £50,000

   Variable element per unit = £50,000/100,000 = £0.5 per unit

   Flexed budget variable element 120,000 × £0.5 = £60,000

   Total flexed cost = £22,000 + £60,000 = £82,000

5. Budgeted marketing cost is stepped, but original and flexed budget in the same range so flexed budget = £180,000.

Task 8

| To | Managing Director | Date | (Today) |
| From | Budget Accountant | Subject | Variances for the year ended 30 June 20X6 |

Variances and action to be taken

The variances experienced have been calculated using a flexed budget, meaning that none of the variances are due to differences in the actual volumes sold or produced compared to the budget.

Sales revenue

The adverse variance is due to the reduction in sales price. It is not due to a change in volume for the reasons stated above. This suggests a 5.5% drop in sales price. If the selling price will continue at this reduced level, the standards should be adjusted when preparing the next budget.

Materials

There is only a very small variance in respect of materials costs. However, action has been taken in respect of materials during the year, which suggests that there may be two conflicting factors here.

The loss of the prompt payment discount would mean that the price of materials was more than expected. This would lead to an adverse variance. However the bonus scheme introduced to discourage materials wastage appears to have had a positive effect in reducing materials usage, so counteracting the effect of the increased price.

The materials standard cost should be amended if the bonus scheme is having such an effect and is likely to continue next year. If the cash flow problems were a one-off, then the materials price should not be adjusted in the standard ie it is assumed that the prompt payment discount will be available in future.

Labour

The bonus scheme will have increased the cost of labour, and may be the reason for the adverse labour variance. However, the efficiency of workers should also be considered to see if there has also been an adverse change here. Alternatively, the bonus scheme may be increasing efficiency, in which case the cost of it is causing a very large variance. The cost of the bonus scheme must be weighed up against reduced materials usage and any increased labour efficiency.

Marketing and PR

There is a favourable variance here due to the cancellation of the advertising campaign and also because no sales and marketing director's salary has been paid for part of the year. The stoppage of personal expenditure by the former director will have also reduced the marketing costs.

There is no major variance in depreciation or administration.

Notes